FIX YOUR CREDIT SCORE

HOW TO REPAIR YOUR BAD CREDIT REPORT QUICKLY USING METHODS OF CERTIFIED CONSULTANTS (BONUS: 15 CREDIT DISPUTE LETTERS THAT WORK)

Table of Contents

Introduction

Credit is a part of our everyday life that we have grown so accustomed to that it is impossible to talk about it without paying special attention to the problems that come with it. Not only does the banking language seem complicated, but when people find themselves confronted with the issue of "bad" credit, they either ignore it and carry on without thinking about the consequences or they want to fix it but have no idea how.

When you have a bad credit rating, it can affect not only your ability to obtain a loan. It may also result in problems in terms of securing any type of credit. For instance, you may encounter problems when renting a property, paying deposits on your phone lines as well as other utilities, or getting a store financing. As such, it is necessary to pay attention to your credit rating.

Should you find any inaccuracies or discrepancies in your credit report, you can carry out a credit repair by requesting, usually in writing, that the concerned credit bureau conducts an investigation on the disputed items. In your request, you may include a supporting documentation, if available, or simply state your dispute and request for an investigation.

4

If you haven't figured it out by now, everything in this world revolves around your credit score. Unfortunately, due to the current economic DISASTER, it is becoming more and more difficult for people in the US to obtain credit from the credit card companies, lenders, and big banks. This book was written with one purpose in mind, to show you how to manage and improve your already horrible credit score.

Getting yourself in the best possible financial shape is important to your overall success in life. After all, without the right amount of money to support yourself and your family, it's nearly impossible to do everything that you want and that's what life is all about, right? You want to be able to enjoy yourself as much as possible.

Chapter 1: What They Don't Want You To Know

Credit simply refers to the ability to borrow. We all need money to cater for various expenditures in life. However, just like any other economic resource, it is never enough, which means we are limited to what we can do since almost everything nowadays needs money. In this day and age where consumer price rises are quite apparent, it is getting tougher and tougher for the average person to afford a lifestyle. Right from consumer products to services, everything is now extremely expensive and people need to arrange for a bagful of money to lead a normal life. But it is not possible for him or her to arrange for this money through their monthly income alone and many have to rely on some external sources of credit. For instance, without additional or external financing, individuals and corporations cannot expand or grow financially.

It is important that they have some money at their disposal in order to cater for all their monthly/ yearly financial needs. Borrowing is one of the most reliable sources of financing there is available but, of course, it comes at a cost.

If your credit hasn't improved very much, even though you're sure you've followed all the steps correctly, don't give up on trying to improve your credit. There's a number of things you can do, which will at least do some sort of damage control. The consequences of the negative items in your credit report will significantly be reduced. It is easy to get discouraged at this point and skip over the damage control step, but keep in mind that you have to put in some effort. The damage control might come in handy in the future, when you try again to repair your credit. All the information you've collected now will be useful in a future credit repair because some of the problems you've encountered now and that you found out are correct might be outdated (over seven years old) soon or your financial situation may improve over time, giving you more grounds for negotiation. Most importantly, by doing a bit of credit repairing and damage control now, this will give you a better starting point for a future credit repair that will be a lot more successful.

The first thing you must do when you've reached this point is to make another list, with the problems you still have and give brief explanations to each. Letters containing no more than one hundred words each, explaining the reason for which you have that negative item on your credit report, will be attached to your credit report, so that when a creditor evaluates your application for a new credit, he will score it correctly and more in your favor. He now knows what's going on in your life and is looking at more than just bad numbers. The letters will be part of your credit report permanently. Each short letter should say more or less the same three things: something bad happened which caused you to default on your payments, but you have remedied that and bounced back and now you are up to date with everything. It should reflect how your financial behavior has improved and a damage control option might even be enough to get you a positive score on a credit application. Just make sure that, if your creditor is reviewing your report in an electronic format, they know that you have included one or more written statements. If he can't find the letters attached, you should have copies to send or hand them to the person working at the creditor's office that is in charge of your scores.

In this case, I recommend taking legal action. I know what you may be thinking. If you have financial problems, the cost of taking the issue to court will only add to these problems. You don't need a lawyer to take legal action for these issues. You can go to a small claims court with the proof you have gathered and do something about both the creditor and the credit reports agency. This will also entail some research, because the legal procedures involved are quite different from state to state. So make sure that before you go to court you are prepared and brush up on the legislation in the part of the country you're in. If you have been wronged, it's worth the extra effort, especially since it will turn your credit from bad to good.

Others Terms Related to Credit Repair

Credit Report: It will include your personal details like birth date, address, etc. It will also have information about your existing credit which includes any open accounts like credit cards, mortgages, and student and car loans. It will have the terms and how well you paid on those terms as well. Some information from your public record will also be on your credit reports such as any court judgments, bankruptcies, and tax liens you may have against you. Lastly, it will have information on inquiries into your credit.

Credit Score: Your credit score is different yet related to your credit report. Some important things are to be considered when viewing your credit score. These include how many and what types of credit accounts you have or have had in the past, how well you have paid your bills on time, or if you have collections against you or other outstanding debt. This is also called a credit rating.

Consumer: A consumer is someone who is involved in the economy by purchasing goods and services for their personal use. In credit, this term is used to refer to anyone who has a credit report or has credit issued to them by a creditor.

Creditors: These are the companies where you access credit from. A creditor is a company that furnishes information for consumer reporting agencies about consumers that have a credit agreement with them. The Consumer Reporting Agency (CRA): A CRA is any person or business that assembles information on consumers and sells or otherwise engages in disseminating that information for preparing or furnishing consumer reports.

Credit Bureau: These people are responsible for collecting credit data from past and present creditors to then compile reports, which are modeled into credit profiles for every credit consumer. This credit report/profile is then sold to creditors to make different decisions including how much they will charge you for borrowing and how much penalty you should pay if you default. A credit bureau is a type of consumer reporting agency (CRA) that gathers information from creditors and then disseminates that information for use in making credit decisions. The information is also used for some other purposes such as employment.

Tax Lien: Tax liens are legal remedies that your creditors can use to collect payment for your debts from you. If you have a tax lien against you, the IRS has a legal right to your property such as your home, bank accounts, or car.

Charge-off: Charge-offs occur when you are very late paying on a debt account. Usually, a charge-off will show up on your credit report after you have not paid on your account for over 180 days.

Judgments: A judgment is a statement that will show up on your credit report if a court has ruled against you and thus you owe money on a lawsuit. This can happen for a variety of reasons such as unpaid collections. Since judgments are public records, they can be seen by anyone who searches for the information and is easily discovered and collected by credit bureaus for your credit report.

Nothing in this world will be only about benefits and there will be several good things that come with a price. That is, this cost of borrowing is closely tied to the credit score, which determines how high or low your interest will be; different people will pay differently based on their credit score. It will depend on whether they are good candidates to repay a loan on time and whether they have the capacity to pay at all.

Although most companies will have strategies in place to help them repair their score, the same cannot be said about individuals. An individual will have to fend for himself and there won't be others who will rush in to help him and control the damage. Therefore, you need to look after your credit score yourself and make sure that it is always high.

To put it into perspective, your credit score is closely linked to your mortgage, car insurance, life and health insurance, car repayments, utilities, and cell phones just to mention a few of the things closely related to your credit score. So anything that relates to your daily upkeep will also be related directly to your credit score and in order to keep your credit score clean, you will have to pay attention to it and maintain as high a score as possible. Interestingly, employers now check your credit score before hiring. So it is important that you have a good score in order to be ready to start your financial journey.

As you can see, having a messed up credit score will probably make your life as far as finances and access to various products and services a living hell. You will not have a chance to lead a normal life and, in fact, when your credit score is in bad shape, you probably need a miracle to live in your dream house or drive your dream car just to mention some of the things you could probably miss out on.

The moment you finally start to understand the power that good credit can give you, you should see things my way. Most of us only know the feeling of having the weight of the world on our shoulders because of our own financial struggles as we get stuck on the bill paying treadmill and our money is accounted for before we even get it. Waking up in the morning can be hard when you don't see a way out and having a dead-end job, no job or just being broke can discourage anyone and force them to become content with the few options they are given. Bad credit can make you feel like you are not living up to your full potential, it does not feel good cutting corners and always having to find an alternative way when it comes to anything related to using your name and credit. I know this is the reality of a lot of people reading this, but it does not have to stay that way.

In this context, performing would consist of a consumer using a credit card to make purchases.

This is what the card issuer wants consumers to do. The idea of "buy now and pay later" allows most people to enjoy the luxuries of a higher standard of living. How many of us would be able to visit the local Lexus dealer and pay for a new car with spot cash? Not many, I assume. Credit allows us to protract our repayment obligation over a period of time (sometimes defined and other times not), thereby alleviating the burden of responsibility of an immediate debt.

Credit allows us the comfort and convenience of shopping online, via telephone, through catalogs and so on. In fact, in some areas, individuals cannot even receive movie rental memberships without guaranteeing them with a credit card. Rental cars and vehicles used to aid in moving must also be reserved for using credit or debit cards. In this light, credit offers consumers a variety of products and services that would otherwise be inaccessible or at least difficult to enjoy.

Banks and various loan institutions also benefit from the use of credit. While they may not require full payment of debt up front, they earn money from finance charges, over-the-limit fees, late fees (which have gradually increased over time) and other expenses that they impose.

Upon accepting a loan, a consumer is agreeing to

repay a bank for not only the original amount of the loan but also any finance charges that may have been assessed based on his or her credit history and other factors. Financing of most loans is fixed, meaning that it cannot change unless the debt is refinanced.

Credit cards, however, work a bit differently. The annual percentage rates may vary based on various factors, such as the end of a promotion, occurrence of a late payment made by a cardholder, adverse or positive review of a cardholder's credit history by issuing company and so forth.

Some of these factors could result in a consumer receiving a more competitive annual percentage rate than he or she previously had. For example, sometimes we receive letters from our existing banks or credit card providers informing us that they have increased our credit limits due to good payment history. Be wary: a higher credit limit sounds tantalizing, but its primary purpose is to heighten your debt.

Higher credit limits equal higher risks for most consumers. What they do not mention is that they have also reviewed your credit records. This is legal. When we enter into contracts with issuers of credit (meaning, we accept the card), we are giving them the authorization to review our credit histories as often as they would like to during the life of the account. However, do not be alarmed! These types of credit reviews (frequently referred to as "soft inquiries") are not detrimental to your overall credit rating.

Most consumers regard credit as an intricate and confusing concept. This approach is taken because people fear the unknown. Enlightened, educated and well-informed consumers understand how credit works and the importance of it. By **understanding** credit and viewing it in a mutualistic manner, it is not such a bad concept after all. Credit offers both merchants and consumers a variety of benefits.

Knowing you possess the ability and having a chance to take advantage of opportunities will make it a little easier to get out of bed in the morning, but first you must learn how. I am not here to give you a motivational speech or sell you dreams. I am here to let you know that we are all capable of doing so much more than we think we can regardless of the position we are in today. Credit cards work on the basis that they know you wish you had more help, if only you could be in a position to take advantage of certain opportunities that come your way. We all have these types of conversations in our heads, but what will you do about it?

It's simple. Credit is your credibility as related to your name and social security number. Your credibility is built from your own financial borrowing patterns. You can develop creditability within any nation, organization, company or with an individual, but being financially credible as we know it here in America comes from our dealings with lenders, banks and other forms of financial institutions. These financial entities furnish our information to credit agencies and companies that import and then summarized our activities into algorithms, which they use to generate credit scores. These credit agencies - also referred to as credit bureaus - are corporations that store our information in a file to identify our past and current creditability but more importantly they determine our future credit worthiness. Your past behavior will dictate your current credit standing or whether you can be trusted to borrow a small sum, pay it back on set terms and if you can, you will then become more credible. It's that simple.

What is Bad Credit?

Bad credit is when you've missed one or more payments throughout your life, be it your fault or not. The most common mistake people make is not defaulting on a payment. It is actually delaying payments. It is usually when you forget about a deadline or can't find a certain bill and you end up not paying, or being late which, in the eyes of the people lending you money makes you look a bit financially unstable. Sometimes, even if you have behaved impeccably, you can, unfortunately, be affected by the loss of a job. Becoming unemployed has such grave consequences and can lead to your assets being repossessed or even bankruptcy. Even if you went through a similar phase and you've bounced back, having this kind of history will impact your credit report in a negative way for a very long period of time.

It can also happen to you if you are the victim of an error, even if you've not missed a single payment on your credit card until now. An error in the bank's system or an error from the parties responsible for building your credit report will affect you nonetheless, and so will fraud and abuse. Fraud cases are rare, but their consequences are costly. Fraud happens when someone uses your identity to submit a credit application, they get it and then they don't repay it. You will be contacted by the bank and until you can prove you've been the target of a scam, you can have a tough time. Abuse generally refers to when you are oblivious to your expenses and spend over your credit card limit. You can wake up one day to a huge amount of debt and cases of abuse most often end in you being forced to declare bankruptcy. In order to avoid these cases, you need to be very careful with your finances, but regardless of what your situation is, usually there is a solution or a set of measures you can take to prevent it.

How to Avoid Bad Credit

First of all, if you have lost your main source of income and are not able to make your payments on time or at all, it is important to say so. Announcing the fact that you may be unable to pay in the next couple of months might land you a grace period from the lender. That means that you will not suffer any penalties for a given period of time, until you can get back on your feet, maybe get a new job and you can resume your normal payments.

The next step is a bit harder, as you have to prioritize bills, meaning you'll have to make a few judgment calls on what bills you should pay with the money you have left and which ones might be less likely to affect your credit. Keeping up with your bills is difficult, but it is also important if you don't want to end up with bad credit. Use your savings or whatever else you have available and you may be able to make your credit look good even if you went through losing your job. These methods work to prevent bad credit, but they also apply in the case of you doing damage control. A credit repair will be a lot easier if you benefitted from a grace period and don't have as many past due bills. It shows you were concerned and aware of the situation and that you tried your best to remain in control of your finances.

Establishing Positive Credit Lines

Most banks require you get a minimum of $300 on the card. We got 2. Now, leading up to this I spoke to many lenders, banks, credit repair companies and all of them told me to keep the debt less than 30-33%. We charged each card 50-75 a month of our 300 in credit. Now, where it conflicts is a bank will tell you to pay the balance in full to build your credit and it doesn't make a difference, your credit will climb. Almost everyone else told me to leave a bit left on the balance, that it does help credit scores climb higher. When you get your statement it has a minimum balance that will be less than $10 if you charged $50. So we paid 40.

Chapter 2: What Is A Credit Score?

Credit simply means your ability to borrow. As such, your credit score is a numerical representation of the risk a lender faces if they were to lend money to you. It is based on the analysis of one's credit files/history. Another layman's definition is that it is the difference between being denied credit and being granted credit. Well, since money is often scarce, borrowing becomes a great option for sourcing funds to do whatever you want to do. It simply enables you to do things you would otherwise not afford if you were to be paying in cash. The credit score determines how lenders perceive you when advancing credit. When your score is high, it means you are a reliable borrower so you won't need to pay more but when the score is low, the lenders treat you with caution and charge you more to advance credit to you. The cost of borrowing (interest you pay) is usually linked to your credit score. In other terms, the credit score determines how much you pay for a mortgage, health insurance, car insurance, and lots of other things including your utilities, cell phones, car payments, etc. Employers also look into credit scores lately before hiring, which means this can determine whether you are hired or not. As you may have noticed, if your score is not good, your life can be pretty much a nightmare. You will probably not even fathom the idea of living in your dream home, or driving your dream car because getting these will be literally out of your reach. Don't get me wrong, these people that run from their debts are not bad people. Maybe they have a reason to stop paying off their debts. While a few missed payments may seem harmless, it actually does you permanent damage.

This damage becomes apparent when you try to borrow money from lenders, or when you get a new credit card. The fact that you missed some payments is permanently reflected on your credit score.

The Purpose of Credit Scores

Credit scores are designed to mitigate various types of risk. The most commonly mentioned risk is that of lending money to a borrower. It determines one's credit worthiness *i.e.* how lending money to you is risky. Here is a summary of why credit scoring is great.

- Credit scores allow people to get loans

faster (almost instantly) since lenders can speed up the approval process. It is possible to make instant credit decisions if you are a lender, which means this helps borrowers to access credit fast.

- It is an objective way of making credit decisions: This focuses on facts rather than feelings which are unverifiable.

- There is more credit: Lenders approve more loans based on credit.

- Lower credit rates: There are more lenders (credit), which increases competition thus pushing the cost of credit lower.

Why should your credit score be high?

- Cheaper credit: Lenders are more willing to offer a lower interest rate. Here is a practical scenario:

- A credit score of 750 translates to a 6.11 interest on a 30 year $300,000 mortgage, while a credit score of 620 translates to a 7.42 interest on the same mortgage. As you can see, this difference will definitely translate into thousands of dollars over the 30-year mortgage period.

- It puts you on an equal footing with

creditors and lenders. You can comfortably negotiate knowing that lenders are competing to have you as their good risk borrower.

- In addition, businesses develop interest in your business because it is a high value asset courtesy of the low risk.

- Insurance companies also request your credit report before deciding your premiums or even whether they will cover a risk for you.

How a Credit Score is Calculated

Your FICO score is a measure of the overall quality of your credit. While it is not the only available metric for determining credit score, it is the one that is most commonly used by a wide range of different lenders and companies when it comes to determining the level of risk that is associated with a given individual.

The calculations that go into determining a person's credit score are proprietary which means that the Fair Isaac Company doesn't share them with anyone. However, some of the details regarding it have been found out, including the fact that a FICO score is based on a handful of different categories at various levels of importance to the total. It has been determined that payment history is weighted with approximately 35 percent relevance, the amount owed has a 30 percent relevance, credit history length has a 15 percent relevance, abundance of new credit has a 10 percent relevance and the type of credit used has a 10 percent relevance.

Payment history relates to how prompt you have been when it comes to previous payments you have made to various creditors. It also factors in things such as delinquency, number of accounts you have in collections, bankruptcy and how long it has been since these problems appeared on your record. As such, the greater number of problems you have had in this regard, the worse your overall FICO score is going to be.

When it comes to the amount you currently owe to lenders, FICO takes into account the amount of debt you currently have as well as the types of accounts you hold and the number of different accounts that you currently hold.

Chapter 3: What Is In Your Credit Report?

To start off, there are probably several things on your report that you will not understand. That is okay. Be sure to obtain the reports directly from the bureaus, not from a bank. This is because the ones from the bank are written for the lenders. They will not have all of the information that you, who the report is about, will need. A lender's copy from the bank will instead show you information that you will not need like the creditor's member numbers while leaving out things like a list of every company that has bought and seen the report which is useful to you.

The next section will be your credit history. Sometimes, you will see "tradelines" listed in this section. Those are the individual accounts in your history. This number may be scrambled as a security measure for the creditor. Sometimes, you will see more than one line or account for a single creditor which is fine. Moving or transferring accounts is common.

Each entry in your credit history will include the following information about it:

- Which kind of credit it was (examples could be revolving credit lines like cards versus mortgage or car loans).

- If this is only a line of credit to you or if it is shared with someone else. Large items like a mortgage or business loan are often shared with a spouse, family member, friend, or business partner.

- The total amount of the credit or the credit limit.

- How much is still owed out of that limit?

- How much the monthly payments are.

- If the account is open, inactive, paid off, or closed.

- How reliably you have paid on the credit account.

In addition to this information, your recent payment history is also included. This will show if you have paid the agreed amount each month and the amount of the payments. This section will show if you have closed an account, it went to collections, if it is charged off or if it is in default. A charge off means that the creditor has given up on getting you to pay your debt. This is not a good thing to have on your credit report.

FIX YOUR CREDIT SCORE

For each entry on your credit history section, the contact information for each line of credit will also be shown. Take note of this information as it will be useful if you ever have disputes or problems with your creditor.

The third section is public records. These include only the financial data of your records which includes tax liens, judgments, wage garnishment, and bankruptcies. Things like if you have been arrested or had a lawsuit brought against you will not be in your credit report. This really is not a good section to have information in since it always shows that you have had a problem with your finances.

In other sections you may find consumer reports, which are short and voluntary explanations for something in your report. Also included is a separate list of all accounts that are in collections, a list of any disputes you have made and if they have been corrected, with an abridged version of individual entitlements as stated by the act and law of your state law. The sections can be used to your benefit. Be sure to keep the copy of your rights on file for easy access.

Things that are not on your credit report and are not collected by the credit bureaus are a record of bounced checks, your race or ethnicity, sex or gender, income, or political views. Some information is kept by the credit bureaus but is not going to show up on your credit report so as to avoid any negative hits to your report. The report is no longer going to show up old and paid debts since they are older than the required time limit.

Chapter 4: How the Credit System Works

In a nutshell, the entire credit system constitutes the credit bureaus, the creditors and you. Creditors are the companies you access credit from while the credit bureaus collect credit data from past and current creditors and compile it into reports, which are modeled in the form of credit profiles for each credit consumer, after which they sell these reports to creditors so that they can make various decisions.

The creditors use the data they obtain from credit bureaus to determine how much they will charge you for borrowing and the amount of penalties they should charge you for defaulting. Whenever a creditor needs credit profiles of people that have a certain credit score, they buy that information from the credit bureaus. This helps them to target their products and services since they will then send emails to those in that list enticing them to buy or use their products and services. It is believed that most of these companies go after those that have a low score. This will allow them to have a chance at making a greater profit and pulling out as much money as possible from these people's pockets.

The credit system consists of three parties namely you, the creditors, and the credit bureaus.

If a creditor needs a report of credit consumers who have a specific credit score, they can then buy the credit profiles from the credit bureaus thus making it easy to target products and services appropriately. They (creditors) will send you enticing information on offers that you should buy.

Subprime credit data is actually the best-selling for the different credit reporting agencies. This is why if you have a subprime credit rating. You are likely to be getting countless email solicitations for you to apply to different credit cards. The reasoning for this is pretty straight forward. With a subprime credit rating, you are definitely going to be charged more for accessing credit. This simply means that the lenders will make more money from you. If you have excellent credit rating, you are low risk and lenders charge you less for accessing credit, which means that they make less money when they advance your credit. In other terms, lenders will want to prey on you if you have bad credit because they are certain that they will make more money in the end. Even if you are to default, you are likely to have paid more money than someone who has good credit! Subprime data is such a hot selling product that the credit reporting agencies charge more for it; it is in high demand! This can be translated to mean that the creditors and credit bureaus don't care about you having good credit. In any case, if your credit rating is bad, they will charge you more! Do you know that over 90 percent of credit reports have been proven to have inaccurate, unverifiable, and erroneous entries?

Well, now you know why your credit score is always becoming bad even with all your effort. These companies are in it for profit. They will even overlook when erroneous entries are posted in your report. In any case, they have convinced us to think that the reports are the gospel truth when they actually are nowhere close to that. So, in simple terms, these 2 players in the credit system can only be compelled by the law to put things in order. They have no interest in you having perfect credit because they all make more money if you have bad credit.

If you are in this group of credit consumers, you will get the most enticing offers and email solicitations to apply for credit cards. The reason is simple, as was mentioned, when your credit score isn't so good, the creditors will definitely charge more for advancing your credit, which means that they make more money. In financial terms, creditors address their exposure to credit risk through charging more for credit. If you have the capacity to pay the right amount on time this will cause them to lose out on a substantial amount of profit. They will not be satisfied with what they receive and will want more out of their customers. They might not directly refuse you credit but will not be particularly interested in giving you money. They will be waiting for someone with bad credit to walk in. Actually, when you have poor credit, you might be paying up to three times what you would pay were you to have a perfect credit score.

So the companies will expressly go after those that have a bad score and will put in all possible effort to trap them. As you can see, creditors will definitely be inclined to prey on those with sub-prime credit score for the simple reason that they will make more money from them even if they were to default as they will have made money already! So there is a lot of planning that they do just to fill up their pockets.

It should not surprise you that these companies work hand in hand. It takes effort from both ends for their schemes to work and they will ensure that they are on the same page. They will come up with plans that will benefit both and cause each to make a large profit at the expense of the customer. Imagine trying to cheat millions of customers on a yearly basis, it is a Herculean task and will require the company to be as prepared as possible to pull it off with ease. For this reason, they will join hands and make sure each one cuts into the profit.

Apart from these 2, there will be some third parties who will work to help these credit companies. These can be outsourced companies or independent ones looking to hook up with the credit companies and trying to make money for themselves. These will have the exclusive job of looking for people that have not checked their records for some time and determine to get them on board. They will put in a lot of effort to catch these people's fancy and once they trap them, they will direct them to the credit company and get them to pay for their services.

To prove that your bad credit history records are a best seller for credit reporting agencies, do you know that they will even charge more to credit providers to access such information. That's right, they will pay up a little extra just to find those that have a bad credit and start bombarding them with emails that ask them to apply for credit at their place. This means that none of these parties has any specific interest to have the information in your credit report reported accurately.

Do you know that only a small percentage of people actually file disputes for such items despite over 90 percent of credit reports having been found to have erroneous, unverifiable and inaccurate entries? Many will not wish to go through the pain of proving themselves right. This allows the companies to have a long leash and they will not back away from exploiting these people. The companies have several good field days owing to such ignorance on the part of the customers.

The credit companies will be determined to report your bad credit and this means that some of them will even let such entries be included in your credit report for the simple reason that so few of us have the guts to challenge entries in the credit report even if they are incorrect, unverifiable and erroneous. They will know who exactly will not challenge it just by looking at your credit history. They will not have an interest in catering to those that might take up a dispute. They will employ people to especially look for those customers that have a bad score and those that look most likely to remain mum about errors in their reports.

The 2 other players in the credit system (the creditors and the credit reporting agencies) are in it to make the most money from you directly or indirectly so counting on them to help you make things right should be out of the question. Actually, the more screwed up your credit score is, the more money there is to be made by the credit reporting agencies and the creditors. That is, the lower the score, the better their prospects to charge you a bomb.

So, when you file a dispute, the creditors and the credit reporting agencies will only update the data - not because they have any interest in your welfare - but because they don't have an option given to them and they are under legal obligation to act in accordance with the law. They will not expressly pursue your cause and, in fact, despite your efforts to fix your bad score, they will try and remain ignorant of it and make things worse for you. They will go to any lengths just to make sure that you have no chance of fixing your score despite none of it being your fault.

This is the exact reason why there are hundreds, probably thousands, of people who despise credit card companies. They will not stop at anything and fall to the absolute lows just to make a few extra dollars. Many of these companies will have a bad reputation and yet find easy prey for themselves. They will know how exactly they can target the customers and get them to subscribe to their card. Once the person is trapped, they will not stop until they fulfill their desire to make as much money as possible. The poor customer will be trapped and will have to surrender to the demands of the vicious company.

Every day, there are hundreds of innocent customers who fall for this trick and do not put in the effort to check their credit reports. But it is important for every person to thoroughly go through their report and look for any erroneous and wrong entries that may be causing them their low scores.

Now that you understand that no one but yourself is on your side on matters pertaining the accuracy of the credit report, how do you know how your credit score affects your ability to borrow? It is apparent that your score is the most vital element in your report and something that needs to be looked into carefully. But what is this score and what are its parameters? How do you know that your score is good, average or bad?

Of course the report doesn't state that a certain amount is bad, so understanding what benchmarks the lenders are going to use in categorizing you as good (perfect), average (sub-prime) and bad will be very helpful so that you know what to expect when you see that number on your credit report.

Chapter 5: Is Your Credit Score Good or Bad?

Your credit score could range from anywhere between the low 300s to mid-800s. These are the general score ranges that are considered by credit bureaus and credit companies. It should be apparent from this that the 800 mark is the highest and the 300 is the lowest.

As you already know, having a poor credit score will determine how much it costs for you to access credit. The lower it gets, the worse your interest rates and the more money you will spend. However, we looked at how companies will flock to target you and try and get as much money out of you as possible. These figures are set based on calculations that are done by the credit bureaus. Depending on your credit history, they will add up your debts and come up with a number that will help determine where you stand.

To help you understand the scores better, here is a breakdown of the credit score ranges and what each means. You will probably find that your credit score is worse than you thought!

720 and Above-Excellent

When you have this score, you get the best interest rates and repayment terms for all loans. This score can come in handy if you are hoping to make some major purchases. You will be able to get credit without any problems and at the lowest possible rates. But then, this score is extremely hard to establish. You will have to put in a lot of effort to maintain this score and still, you will not come anywhere close to 800. The most you can wish to come close to is 720 and remain there for as long as possible.

680-719-Good

When you are in this category, you will get good rates and terms but not as good as those with excellent scores. With this score, you can get favorable mortgage terms. You might not face as many problems but will have to be ready to run around from company to company to have your credit approved. Again, this score is not very common. You need to put in extra effort to get it over the 680 mark. If because of some erroneous charges you are not able to cross this limit then you must try your best to get it cleared as soon as possible.

620-679-Average

When you are in this category, you can get fair mortgage terms and have it easy when buying smaller ticket items, (of course with no better rate than good and excellent scores). Take care not to slip down to the level where mortgage is unaffordable.

580-619-Poor

When you are at this level, you only get credit on the lenders' terms. You will probably pay more to access credit so be ready to pay more. Also, you should remember that you cannot access auto financing if your score goes lower than this range so you should work towards building it. This is where a large majority lie. Their score will be bad mostly owing to wrong entries. If you lie here then you will have a tough time getting credit in your budget limits and will have to be ready to pay up a lot of money.

500-579-Bad

If your credit score is in this range, access to credit will cost you dearly. Actually, if you are looking for a 30-year mortgage, you could be looking at, at least 3% higher interest rates than how much you would pay if you had good credit. On the other hand, if you are looking for something short time like a 36-month auto loan, you will probably pay almost double the interest rate you would pay if you had good credit. So being here is probably the worst thing that can happen to your credit report. You cannot possibly be here and hope to get away with low interest rates. That is next to impossible.

Less than 500

If your credit score goes to this level, it is so bad that it might be almost impossible to get any type of financing. If you do, the interest rate will simply be unfathomable. You might have to spend 30 to 40 years trying to repay it. Your entire life will be dedicated toward repaying a loan and you might only get free by the time you are 50.

I am sure several of you are in this last range. But don't panic as help is at hand. You might wonder if it is possible for you to fix your score if you are in this category and the answer is yes! It is possible for you to improve your credit score and possibly enter the good range.

How Credit Report Mistakes Are Made

Understand that no one wants to have his or her credit score bad for the simple reason that access to credit will be too costly. It will be the worst type of score for any person to have regardless of their borrowing habits. That's why it is paramount to take action when you start seeing inaccurate and unjustifiable entries in your report. If you spot errors that are causing you to be in this range, then you must spring into action at the earliest opportunity. To help you understand what's at stake here, let me explain to you in detail why you should start following up on everything reported on your credit report. Otherwise you might end up paying more for credit than you ought to and you don't have to learn the hard way.

For instance, a change in the date of the last activity on your credit report should be something you should start worrying about. When you have something derogatory appearing in the recent activity items, your credit score will be tainted. This might be completely imaginary or a simple manipulation of your actual entry. You may even have noticed different creditors reporting the same debt multiple times in which case, your credit report will show that you are really sinking into debt even if this is not actually true. These might show some extra-large values, which will only make your score appear bad. You might also have noted the same creditor reporting the same debt in your credit report under various account numbers. This has the same effect as having multiple creditors reporting on the same debt.

Obviously, creditors could defend themselves as not knowing that these mistakes existed. However, they really don't care less about that because the worse your credit score is, the more they charge you for credit. As was said before, they will stoop to any low just to get you in a fix. They will not care about your side of the story and stick to what they think is their right. So you need to be alert all the time, and do what is right for you.

The law requires that creditors can only keep information about your credit history for 7 years. However, it isn't uncommon for lenders to keep this information for more than 10 years, which means such items will probably continue showing on your credit report year in year out which, in turn, messes your credit score after which the lenders raise the interest rates you pay. They will not be accountable to anyone and will claim to have erased any information in regard to your credit scores. But they will keep using the data to bombard you with target specific mails and offers.

The answer to these inaccuracies in credit reports lies not in sitting around and expecting your creditors to have mercy on you, because they won't. This is the problem that most people suffer from. They think the creditor will empathize with them and help them reduce their bad credit. But they will, in fact, be much more interested in ruining your credit score further so that they have a chance to pull more money from you. So, the best idea is to start doing something about bettering your score and not wasting any more time.

In any case, why do these corporations (lenders) want you to pay them for something you shouldn't pay? You must understand how these companies will try and trick you and remain alert. If at any time you find out you are being cheated owing to mistakes and errors in your credit report, you need to spring into action and deal with them at your earliest convenience. But what must you do to repair your credit as soon as possible?

Knowing you have the right to dispute and actually disputing successfully are two totally different things. I will teach you what to do throughout the process if you are to emerge successful in the dispute process.

So it is vital for you to start doing the right things and move in the right direction to have your score fixed. To start with, you need to start going through every detail in your credit report if you want to know what entries are derogatory in the first place. This means doing a thorough perusal to find what is wrong with your credit report. There could be a lot of errors and you need to look at each and pinpoint them. You can then easily have them rectified. But you can't do that if you don't have up to date reports. You need to have all the reports that will clearly show all your entries. But where should you go to get these updated results? Well, let's take a look at where and how to get them.

Chapter 6: The Advantages of Having a High Credit Score

Because of the formulation of the credit report, banks and lenders find it easier to assess information on the capacity of an applicant to pay for loans. Credit reports show objectivity and consistency. For loan applicants, having a high score will mean advantages.

These days, society is increasingly dependent on credit scores when it comes to making a wide variety of different decisions about your future. Your credit score can vacillate from 350, indicating you are an extremely high-risk investment, to 850, which indicates anyone who loans you money is almost certain to get it back. Additionally, your credit rating is typically shown via a numerical rating from 1 (very bad) to 9 (very good). Currently only about five percent of Americans have a credit rating of 500 or lower while about fifteen percent have a score above 800 with the majority falling between the 700 and 800 range. Here are the benefits of having a high credit score:

Living arrangements

A poor credit rating can prevent you from successfully getting a mortgage at all, or even prevent landlords from renting to you as well. This is due to the fact that many landlords consider a lease a type of loan. After all, they are loaning you a place to live in exchange for rent each month. If you have a low credit rating, and they do decide to rent to you, be prepared to pay extra for the privilege of having a roof over your head.

Car payments

In this case, bad credit can limit your options as fewer lenders will be willing to work with you and those that do are generally going to charge more to balance out the risk you represent. This typically translates into repayments for longer periods of time (72 months as opposed to 60 or less) and higher overall payments each month.

Job searches

While the first two scenarios are to be expected, many people will be surprised to learn that a low credit score can affect your employment prospects as well. While employers can't check credit scores, they can check credit reports and many do so as a routine part of the hiring process. Depending on the job, if you have a history of poor financial responsibility an employer may be hesitant to offer you the position you have been dreaming about. Likewise, when it comes to promotion, many companies check credit reports to ensure their executives won't give the company a bad name.

Starting a business

If you are looking to start a business with a small business loan, then you can bet lenders will check your credit score and, as most new businesses tend to fail, they will be very selective about who they lend their money to.

Monthly bills: Your credit score will also have an effect on many of your monthly bills including your utilities. Utility companies loan you their services every month and if your credit report shows that you are a risky investment, then they will most definitely charge you more for the privilege of having electricity, running water, cellular service or cable and internet.

No matter what race you are, where you were born, where you live, or who your parents are, it doesn't even matter what occupation you are in -

your name in itself is worth money. How much money your name will be worth is solely up to you, your way of thinking and the knowledge you pursue. Other advantages are as follows:

- Better job opportunities
- Easily getting any job
- No requirement for security deposits
- No security deposit for cell phone contracts
- Satisfactory car insurance rates
- Less hassle acceptance in apartments and rental houses
- Approval of loans that have higher limits
- Enhanced negotiating power
- Approval of loan and credit card applications
- Low interest rates for different loans
- Get funds to start or grow your business.
- You will have access to money for emergencies.
- You can qualify to buy a home and build equity.

- Borrow unsecured money for college.

- Access to reward programs that offer free travel.

- Zero or low interest auto loans.

- No deposits on utilities and some leases.

- Qualify for job opportunities that require decent credit and save thousands on insurance policies each year.

- Purchase protection from merchants.

- Travel protection and zero liability rental car insurance.

Chapter 7: Fixing your Credit like a Pro

If you are affected by bad credit, remember it happens to a lot of people. Credit repair will require a lot of effort and it is a process that can span out over the course of many months, but in the end it's worth it. It's possible that a credit repair will not make all your financial problems go away and you may still be confronted with some bad credit "symptoms" that will stay on your credit report. These problems usually require long term attention, but can be minimized over time so much so that even if you have or had them, your credit will still be considered good. I will try to explain credit repairing as best as I can so that it can be accessible to everyone

The first step for fixing your credit is doing your homework. This involves a bit of research, but it can be done in a few hours or days, depending on the time you allocate daily to this problem. What you must do is get copies of your credit reports from more than one agency. Two or three are the best option. Compare your credit reports and pick out the problems you find that are important

51

or predominant. After you identify what causes your credit to be in such bad shape, try to write down why each negative point is the way it is. The importance of correctly identifying the problems cannot be stressed enough. Once you find out what led to the negative items in credit reports, try to reason with yourself. Why should each one of them be eliminated? With a clear motive and a clear perspective on each problem, a lot of the work is already done and you can move on to searching for solutions. These will come more easily since you now know what your bad credit is based on and why you need to remove certain problems. Setting clear and realistic goals is a step that is widely used in fixing any problem, not just financial difficulties.

You may find that some of the issues in the credit reports may be incorrect or have already been remedied, in which case you should contact the agency that put together your credit report and explain your point of view. Reporting agencies can't know what happens in your life on a daily basis and even though they keep an updated database, it takes time to do it so they will appreciate your clarification. Keep in mind that you have to make time to do some investigative work of your own. But how will I be able to analyze all this information correctly if I don't have any experience in finance? Not all reports will look the same, which is why you should be provided with the necessary information to decode them. You should pay special attention to the fields which show which payments are up to date, defaulted or late, because there you will also find the reason why they've inserted each negative entry. You should also pay special attention to the time the account was opened, information on monthly payments and credit limit. Of course, any incorrect information will easily be corrected and if that scratches a few items off your list, that's a happy case.

Follow these Strategies to Fix your Credit

Delete inquiries

In this strategy, you agree to pay a creditor only if they agree to delete such items from the credit report. I mentioned zero balances; don't fall for the trap of creditors who say they will mark it as zero. Zero is not good for you because it shows you have been having problems in the past (this sticks in your credit report for 7 or more years)! If the information passes to collection agencies after 2 years, you can also use this strategy to make them stop reporting your settled debt. In any case, they buy the debts for a tiny fraction so anything they get will probably be good enough! This is the best time (when the debt is with the collection agencies) to use the pay to delete strategy because you have more bargaining power. If the collection agency doesn't accept your offer, its only option is through a judgment.

Note#1: Use pay to delete when you start noticing new derogative items in your report since these could easily hurt your credit. You might even start seeing multiple collection companies reporting the same debt. In such times, you have an advantage since you negotiate everything on your terms; if one does not accept your offer, another will definitely take it.

Note#2: Have everything put in writing if they agree on your terms. If they cannot put it in writing, don't pay. After paying, you should give it about 45 days to reflect in your credit report. Don't take anything less than deletion. Don't accept updating the balance. If they cannot delete, don't pay. The process is pretty fast so they shouldn't give you excuses that they cannot delete. Mention the Universal Data Form to let them know that you know that it is possible.

Note#3: Choose your battles well *i.e.* Do not use this strategy on creditors who have a lot to lose because they might sue you to compel you to pay.

Aim for creditors who have already been barred by the statute of limitation (2 years have passed), which means they cannot sue you in court to compel you to pay.

Identify theft claim

This is definitely a large population so anyone could be a victim. If you are sure that your score has been ruined because of identity theft, you can use this method. Abusing this method could land you into trouble with the law. Here is how to dispute using the method:

- Step 1: Report to the police because you will need this report later

- Step2: File the dispute with FTC using this link *here*.

- Step 3: Go on to dispute with various credit bureaus.

- Step4: Set up an identity theft alert (be sure to know what this means in terms of your access to credit).

Lookout for errors in the report

I mentioned that 93% of credit reports have been proven to have errors. Look out for any of these then file a dispute. Such things as the last date of activity, write off date, wrong account name or number and others could be enough to taint your credit. Don't overlook any of that. If the report really has an error, don't be discouraged by the credit bureau's stalling tactics. Mention the Notice (Summons) and complaint to let them know that you are really aware of what the law requires of them. The bureaus wouldn't want to have their systems investigated and proven to be weak/flawed so this strategy can actually compel them to correct errors thus boosting your credit.

Pay the original creditor

You don't want multiple collection agencies reporting new items every month since this hurts your score. Simply send a check with full payment of the outstanding amount to the original creditor. Then send proof of the payment to the collection agencies that have reported that debt. After that, you then request that they should delete all the derogatory items from your credit report. You can blend this with the pay to delete strategy mentioned above.

Request for proof of the original debt

If you are sure that the credit card has been written off due to late payment, there are times when the carriers might not have the original billing statements within 30 days as stipulated by the law. With this, you can get the item removed from your report so that it appears as if the entry was never there. You can also request the original contract that you actually signed when applying for a credit card.

Settle your debt

Total debt owed accounts for up to 30% of the credit score so don't overlook this. This includes personal loans, car loan, and credit utilization. You should also calculate the credit utilization ratio (the balance you carry in your revolving fund compared to your credit). To pay your debts, you can use snowballing or avalanching strategies. Snowballing involves paying off debts with the lowest balance first then closing them as you move up to the bigger debts. Avalanching involves paying debts starting from those with the highest interest rates as you move down.

Settle your bills promptly

You could even set up automatic payments just to ensure that you won't miss payments since the amounts are deducted from your account. The biggest contributors to this include collections, bankruptcies, and different late payments. You should note that the recent delinquencies have a greater effect than old ones; 70% of the score is determined by whatever has happened within the past 2 years.

Contact with the creditor

At this point, you have to write another letter, this time to the creditor. You can continue claiming that the negative information is wrong, but be warned that they will not believe you if you do not provide solid proof to back up your claim. If you don't think you can muster up that proof in order to make a good case for re-establishing your good credit, I suggest you consider a different route. You can write to the creditor and express the fact that you are concerned about the issue affecting your good credit and even though you are aware that the negative item is based on accurate facts, you want to find a solution that will work for both parties involved. This way, you announce your intent of repairing your credit in a polite and professional way, so they might be more predisposed towards collaborating with you in finding a more suitable solution.

Handling Disputes for Delinquent Accounts

The main methods of improving your score from this point involve disputing and removing negative information, and managing your current credit accounts. If this is your first look at this, chances are that you have a few incorrect items showing up on one of your reports. That is not a problem because we are going to get them removed! Everyone is entitled to dispute incorrect information on his or her credit report, and by law the credit bureau has to look into it in a timely manner (usually 30 days.) Now if this is an account that shows an amount due but actually has a zero balance, you can always get it removed from your record. Occasionally you may have to get proof of a zero balance, but this is rare.

Ok, so gather all the incorrect information in front of you. Remember that this can be anything, from misspelled names, to incorrect dates or amounts. There are two methods of disputing, and people will recommend either one.

Your options are to file a dispute online, or mail a dispute letter by certified mail.

Filing a dispute online is simple and quick, which is why I prefer it. You can file many disputes in a short period of time. In fact, "credit repair" companies will usually just dispute everything, hoping the creditors simply don't respond with the correct information. How far you want to take this tactic is completely up to you. Disputes can usually be filed at the same time, and must be done individually with each bureau showing incorrect information.

On each bureau's website, find the online dispute button and follow the instructions. After you pick the appropriate items to dispute, enter the correct information, usually with a brief description of what you are disputing, and when you are done you will be provided with a reference/dispute number. Write this number down! You will need it to check back in on your report and make sure the dispute is removed.

Tracking Your Credit Progress

Before you go out in the world and start applying for more credit, let's get a better idea of your numerical score. There are two easy ways to do this for free. The first is to sign up for *www.creditkarma.com*. It is free and quick, just put in your standard info. It is not necessary to link your checking accounts or any bank information to use the service, but it is offered as a financial management tool if you desire it.

With Credit Karma, be aware that this is not an exact score, it is an estimation based on the data that the website has available. You may notice it is normally accurate, but sometimes it is off by just a little, or lags by a week or two. The actual FICO score itself can vary by as much as 20-50 points, but is normally within 20 points or so. Use Credit Karma as a guide more than anything.

There are a number of other free sites that are similar, but do not quite offer the scope of services that Credit Karma does. You are welcome to explore them all, just be wary of entering credit card or bank information.

The other way to get your numerical credit score is through credit card services. At the time of this writing, a few major banks offer your FICO score through having a credit card account with them, including Barclays, Discover, and Capital One. This is always changing, but the current trend suggests that more companies will start to offer this service.

Pay bills promptly

Most lending companies refer only to payment history in assessing whether a potential borrower is creditworthy or not. As such, to repair his credit score, he must pay his bills immediately, and he must do so promptly and on time. One must remember that a bad payment history decreases the chance that his application will be accepted. Paying his bills promptly also repairs his credit score.

In paying his bills, debts, and obligations, he may choose to consider the following order of priority:

- Pay first those secured by real and personal properties because they can be lost if he fails to pay them on due date.

- Next pay those that have high interest rates to prevent these charges from accumulating over time.

- Next pay those that have high amounts because these require a large amount of money.

- After these three debts are paid, he may choose to divide his remaining money to partially pay his other debts.

Paying bills promptly and on time also increases the length of his credit history because it prevents his accounts from being closed due to delinquency in payment.

Maintain a low debt on credit cards

One must take note that having a high amount of debt decreases the chance that his credit application will be granted. Maintaining a low debt on credit cards also repairs his credit score.

A person can maintain a low debt on credit cards either by paying his bills or by reducing the amount that he spends on his purchases. A suggested practice is for him to pay his credit card bills twice a month and making a list of what he needs to purchase.

Avoid having a high outstanding debt

In relation to maintaining a low debt on credit cards, a person must also avoid having a high outstanding debt because it creates a negative impact on the credit score. To prevent this from happening, he may pay these debts partly based on the amount of money that he has, or he may negotiate with his creditors for possible settlement of these debts.

Most of the time, lending companies accept partial debt payment because it prevents their borrowers from running due to inability to pay. If feasible, it is advisable for him resort to this method so he can slowly decrease his outstanding debt.

Get new accounts only when needed.

A person must get new accounts only when needed and only when his financial resources permit him to do so. Getting many accounts at one time negatively affects his credit score, especially when he has started using a certain amount of credit for each account, because it means that in paying his bills, his financial resources will be divided among these accounts.

Make payment reminders

In promptly paying his bills and debts, a person must make payment reminders. These are small notes that contain various debts that he has to pay, the amount that he needs to spend for every debt, and the frequency through which he needs to make the payment. Making payment reminders helps him a lot in managing his financial resources because it lets him prioritize paying the debt first before allocating his money to something else.

The best time to make payment reminders is when making a budget. A budget is a summary of the sources of revenue and an itemized list of the expenses of a person within a specified period of time, usually for a month. As he lists the items in his budget, he may immediately allocate some of his money in paying his existing debts.

Focus on the credit report. Not the score

Remember, your credit score is just a number, and even though an important number, don't focus on it just yet if you have some repairing or rebuilding to do. Once you get to the point where you have done all you can do to remove anything reporting as derogatory, you will then have the fun part of building or rebuilding your credit. With no negative information and no positive information reporting your score will remain low and it's possible you may have no score at all. We have all heard "No credit is bad credit", but no credit is only a small step away from great credit. Focus on your credit report, it is the determining factor that shows how much you should be trusted, and how much previous creditors have trusted you, this speaks the highest in their decisions.

Maintain a High Credit Score

While doing your credit repair and after achieving a high score, you keep track of the changes, be it progress or decrease. You can ask this from a credit reference agency. This might entail money. Nowadays, there are credit tracking sheets available online for free. You have to make sure that they are trustworthy, though.

Going back to economizing, one way to do this is by using energy-efficient appliances. It is not ideal to buy an appliance based on the price alone. You might be getting an appliance for a low price but you might not have realized that you are getting less than you paid for in terms of quality and reliability. Aside from that, cheaper appliances often consume more electricity. In the long run, you will not have actually saved anything. Aside from saving electricity and money, you have to save water as well. Use only the amount of water that you need.

Preparation is also worth noting in maintaining a high credit score. Unwanted events in the future such as redundancy, moving out, accidents, illnesses, calamities, and death are worth preparing for. You can apply for insurance for these events. Nevertheless, you should still prepare because of the possibility of non-coverage from your insurance premiums.

When it comes to your financial activities, the right attitude would be living in accordance with your financial capacities. Do not be obsessed with materials that you will not be using. Spend your finances for your needs. It does not mean that you should not enjoy your money. As a matter of fact, recreation and rest form part of your needs. All you have to do is to use your money wisely. Treat yourself in a way that you are not incurring debts or lessening your savings.

Chapter 8: How Do Credit Bureaus Operate?

The popular credit bureaus have a significant effect on every consumer, but many people don't know these companies or how they work.

- Experian

- Equifax

- Trans Union

These companies have a great history in the financial industry. Also known as a credit reporting agency, it gathers financial information about consumers and combines this information into a single report. Since these bureaus work independently, the credit report that a single bureau generates for an individual could be slightly different from another bureau's report. Although there are smaller credit bureaus, the top three serve a more significant share of the market.

The credit bureaus have a fascinating profit model. Lenders, banks, and many other companies share a lot of information about their clients with credit bureaus for free. The credit bureaus process this information and put it on sale, in the form of a credit report, to different parties that require insight into your financial history, and more.

Thinking about just one number to represent your credit score is a little too simple. You actually have multiple credit scores, each calculated and maintained by a different company. Usually these scores are very close to each other, but they almost always vary by at least a few points.

The three bureaus are Equifax, Experian, and TransUnion. We will get into the reason that the scores are different a little bit later, but it has to do with the way they collect information. Your score from any of these three companies will be called your FICO../../Downloads/h - _ftn1 score (it may also be a BEACON score from Equifax). If it is called something different, it is just an estimate, and is not the real deal. As we will find out later, that may be ok in some cases, but it is something you should be aware of.

In addition to the three companies, each one actually keeps up to 7 different scores per person. For our purposes, we are just going to focus on what is called the classic or generic score. So from here on out, the words "score" or "credit score" mean the classic or generic score. It is the most commonly used for most purposes (buying a house or getting a loan), and the other scores will follow it up or down for the most part. We aren't worried about two or three points here, we are looking for the biggest changes we can make with the least effort.

Dealing with Credit Bureaus

Today, where the economy is at its weak point, having a good credit is a necessary tool. This is because it allows you to obtain house loans, car loans, credit card, and other convenient financial services and instruments. You may be able to live without having a good credit.

You can discern the credit bureau that holds your file by looking at any rejection letter you received from a recent credit application.

If you are dealing with the credit bureau that handles your file, keep in mind that it belongs in the business of collecting and selling information. As such, you should not provide them with any detail, which is not necessary legally.

When you already have your credit report, make sure to check for any error or discrepancy. If you find anything that is questionable in your report, you can send the credit bureau a written request for them to investigate on the error. In general, the credit bureau has the burden of documenting anything that is included in your credit report. If the credit bureau fails to investigate on the error or neglects your request for an investigation within 30 days, the error should be removed.

You need to educate yourself about the legal obligations of credit bureaus in order to have a successful credit repair process. Prior to dealing with them, make sure you know all the legal aspects so you would not end up paying for something that should not be charged with a fee. Remember, credit bureaus are also businesses and that they own many credit repair companies.

Making the Best of Credit Bureaus

It is a little annoying to learn that all three credit bureaus have sensitive financial data. However, there's no method to prevent lenders and collection entities from sharing your information with the above companies.

You can limit any possible problems associated with the credit bureaus by evaluating your credit reports annually, and acting immediately in case you notice some errors. It is also good to monitor your credit cards and other open credit products to ensure that no one is misusing the accounts. If you have a card that you don't often use, sign up for alerts on that card so that you get notified if any transactions happen, and regularly review statements for your active cards. Next, if you notice any signs of fraud or theft, you can choose to place a credit freeze with the three credit bureaus and be diligent in tracking the activity of your credit card in the future.

How the Bureaus Get Their Information

To learn how the score gets calculated, first we need to learn about all the different inputs of your score, aka where the bureaus get their info. You may have many factors that report information to the credit bureaus, or none.

Credit cards are called revolving accounts or revolving debt by the credit bureaus. Each monthly payment and balance is reported, as well as any late payments. This means that any cards that have your name on them will also report to all the bureaus. This includes cards that belong to a spouse or parent. If you're an authorized user on the account it gets reported on your credit no matter what. Many people have their credit ruined by a spouse or parent going into bankruptcy or not paying their credit card bills. If your name is on any credit cards that belong to people that may not pay their bills, ask them to take your name off immediately!

Installment loans also report information to the credit bureaus. If you went down to your local Sears and financed a washer/dryer set by putting up a down payment, that is an installment loan. The details of these loans are all reported; the total balance, as well as the timeliness and amounts of your monthly payments.

If you have mortgages or student loans, that information does get reported. Total amounts due, total paid so far, and the status of monthly payments is all reported. This information is all kept track of and organized in their databases.

Chapter 9: Dealing with Bankruptcy

Now that we have covered what a credit score is, a note on bankruptcy is in order. The National Foundation for Credit Counseling (NFCC) has some excellent resources on their website for bankruptcy and credit counseling (***https://www.nfcc.org***), and may provide counseling for your situation.

There are other local non-profit organizations that will also negotiate on our behalf to lower your total debt balances. Companies will often negotiate a lower balance if they think that the debtor (that's you) is on the verge of bankruptcy. This should always be considered as an option before bankruptcy, as it does negatively affect your credit, but not as badly as a bankruptcy does.

If you just filed for bankruptcy last week, you will have a very tough time quickly re-establishing credit. If some time has passed, you have a good shot at getting started though. Since bankruptcy is such an individual process, you will have to collect your credit file information and score through the following chapters, and build a plan specifically for your situation. It may be that a little more waiting is required before you can qualify for new credit lines.

If any of this applies to you, please contact the NFCC for additional resources, and please finish this book, as there will be no harm in at least establishing where you stand with your credit. There is an excellent chance you can at least start rebuilding right away. Generally speaking, you can follow through with getting your credit score, and depending on what it is, move forward with establishing new credit as outlined at the end of the book.

The thought of any legal proceedings, judges and the government kept me away from even trying to tackle these items in the past, they just seemed too serious or too big. I also realized a lot of credit experts didn't know how or just didn't attempt to delete a bankruptcy. Understand that some people have filed bankruptcy that included hundreds of thousands of dollars' worth of debt, including foreclosure, auto loans and unsecured lines of credit. I would tell myself, these companies would not allow this to just disappear, if this could be done, everyone would just charge-up debt then file bankruptcy and start all over again. After some research I found out this has been going on with individuals and companies since the 1800s.

Knowing how much the credit agencies depended on 3rd parties to verify items, I then started to work backward and understand exactly how the credit bureaus received and verified the information that they would collect and report relating to any consumer. For any account that is reported, you have to understand from whom and where it came from, and when that item gets disputed you have to know which avenues the credit agencies will use to validate, verify and cross-reference.

Deleting Judgments, Liens, and IRS Tax Liens like the Pros

How to Remove Tax Liens

Tax liens are likely the most serious thing you will find on your credit report and have far reaching consequences. They can lead to tax levies which allow the government to seize your property to satisfy your debts. This can include your bank accounts, retirement accounts, car, personal property such as jewelry and technology, business assets, and home or land.

If this happens to you, be absolutely sure to keep every record you receive involving the lien. If you find any discrepancies, you can file a dispute to have it removed from your credit report. Often times even if you dispute, since it is likely to be a large debt, it still will not be removed from your record. You also cannot avoid a tax lien through bankruptcy as a bankruptcy will not include your tax liens unless it is filed prior to when the lien is placed on your record.

The main way to get a lien off of your record is to pay it off and wait for the seven years period for it to fall off of your record. This is certainly not an ideal situation and thankfully there is a way to remove it from your report if you need to qualify for housing, a car, or other credit.

To remove a lien, you have to request a withdrawal while still making payments using IRS form 12277. You will still have to pay the tax lien completely and pay according to the payment plan. Then you still have to contact both the credit bureaus and the IRS to notify them of the change in your lien status. This is sometimes also possible if it has been paid off already, but you still have to follow the strict guidelines set out by the IRS. Due to the nature of tax liens, a professional will likely be able to guide you through this long and tedious process better than going alone.

Due to recent changes initiated by a coalition of

state Attorney Generals from 31 different states, also consumer advocates, almost half of the tax liens reporting on consumer credit files in this country will be deleted for being incomplete. If the item does not include the following four identifying factors; full name, birthdate, last 4 of social security number and address, it cannot be verified and will be took off of your credit reports. The same thing applies for **CIVIL JUDGMENTS**, a (case file) might exist as a public record, but was the judgment ever correctly recorded? And with all of your information?

This being another small victory against the credit power conglomerates, as they can no longer report restitution as imposed by the courts, including traffic and parking tickets, these collection attempts are penalties and fines, not something you were entrusted to repay or signed-up for. But this is only related to the 3 major credit bureaus, companies like LexisNexis still may report such entries as they do not have to play by the same rules as the credit bureaus. This is why I listed relevant companies in relation to your credit well-being because the credit bureaus use these 3rd parties to do what they can't, I like to call it their dirty work. I advise you to review and suppress as many of these reports as possible. Unlike other items that get furnished onto your credit reports, credit bureaus don't actually get information about public items from the courts themselves. If you have disputed any public item in the past and the credit bureaus informed you that this information was verified by the court, they are lying. The courts, the deeds office, and the county do not report, verify or furnish any information to any credit bureau. Keep in mind, even though this information may be on public record, this still does not mean it was furnished directly to the credit agencies. Privacy laws prevent this from happening, if you send an affidavit to whatever court or county responsible for the judgment, tax lien or bankruptcy asking if they verified or furnished the entry they will respond denying any activity related to furnishing information to credit bureaus by phone, fax, email or mail. The response letter from the court on official letterhead is a weapon to be used against the credit bureaus. Make sure you send copies and keep the original. You have to question their method of verification after an initial dispute was made, but the public item was verified.

The credit bureaus use LexisNexis as a 3rd party to verify any legal information. This is why you need to close this door. Any time you dispute a public item, you have to suppress your report with LN, its related products and affiliated companies. You can request a Suppression form on their website. Only fill out the information that is required and has an asterisk sign by it. If you no longer stay at the address associated with the Item, make sure you submit a suppression form for the address associated with the item, and your current address. Don't supply any information that is not required, don't give them anything extra.

You also want to Freeze Innovis, the 4th lesser known credit bureau, this can be done directly on the website.

Freeze ARS, it stands for "Advanced Resolution Services" which is similar to Innovis, it has to be done with a letter with your signature and a copy of your ID or driver's license.

Now that LN, Innovis, and ARS are all suppressed, and you have closed the access to the verification doors, the only other way for the credit bureaus to actually verify any information regarding your public records will be from PACER.

Chapter 10: How to Handle Student Loans

School is very important, I believe in education but the system does not seem to make much financial sense for anyone who does not have rich parents, receives grants to pay for school or who will be funded by a scholarship. Unknowingly and optimistic, young adults get tricked and persuaded into taking out student loans that may just be the most important decision they will ever have to make, and think about it, most of the time this is at the age of 17 or 18. As a society, we are told that in order for us to become employable and productive in life, we will need a college education; for the majority, if you want to become educated and recognized, you will be forced into debt to attend a university with an accredited program. Just think about it, why can't federal student loans be discharged in bankruptcy?

So what is the solution? I don't have a solution, I am not on a mission to change the system as a whole, but I believe it is no single solution for everyone; each individual will have a different understanding about life and the direction they may want to go. Borrowing money in the form of

81

a student loan may be the only option for some, and for the very focused and determined person, this old system can work out perfectly. How many young adults are fully focused at the age of 18? What they don't tell you before you sign that promissory note and enter in a lifetime agreement via a student loan is, even if you fail to find gainful employment after you finish school, you are still on the hook for the balance. If you don't have financially savvy parents that can explain to you the seriousness of student loan agreements, the universities and your college counselors will not tell you that you might have to live broke like a college student long after entering into the work force. I see too many statistics showing how much more money college graduates will make versus the people who just have a high school diploma or a G.E.D, but nobody ever factors in the years it will take, not just to earn, but to actually pay off the cost of the education. And keep in mind; we haven't even mentioned the effects that recessions might have on the job market of particular career paths. I understand that student loans can be paid off, even those with very high balances but nobody ever explained to students what they would have to sacrifice just to be able to tackle their student loan debt and fight against the compounding interest on a monthly basis.

I really believe if most people really understood how their quality of life would be affected by taking on so much debt so early before earning any money, the education system as we know it would change forever. I challenge any young adult to do some research and spend 7 days listening to the stories of people who just like themselves, eventually became trapped and held down in bondage by their student loan debt. Many young adults go into a college undecided, and may actually end up changing their course of study, or they choose an occupational field of study that may not be able to support their lifestyles while servicing their student loan payments in the future. If the students thoroughly knew at the beginning what they would have to give up, I don't think they would go this route. Fresh-out of high school we typically don't know much about finances, and even though the information is out there, many young people are too consumed with entering into college, picking a major, and dealing with their personal life instead of taking more time to enter into a crash course study of personal finance, this is a failure of preparation not only from parents, but our public high schools.

Unfortunately, for society useful Information on credit isn't being taught at our colleges and universities and it's not by accident. I don't know of any colleges or public high schools that properly teaches and prepares their students for the general knowledge on the uses and responsibilities of credit. The greater concern is getting potential students prepped to borrow money to pay into a business structure called "Higher Learning". I'm not saying college is a bad thing, but if it cost you over $80,000 to complete a degree just to put you in a race to qualify you for a job that starts you off making $40,000, then we have a problem. Just as with anything else in this world, in order for it to make financial sense, you first need to ask yourself, "What is my return on my investment?" You will have to learn to pursue knowledge on your own to get to the top of your field or to live a better life. No one will deliver it to you, they just let you know it exists.

What you can do about student loans

As you may have heard or even have participated in by now, for both Federal and private student loans they have what is called Forbearance and a Deferment option for student loan borrowers. Simply stated, these options will allow your student loans to remain in good standing if they are not already in collections while you catch a break and get your finances in order.

Deferment

A period in which your student loan payments are temporarily put on pause, often for an extended length of time. The federal government and some private lenders will defer your loans if you are currently active in the military or still attending school. Each loan can be different, but you may have an option where you won't have to pay the accumulated interest during this time. Deferments can be retroactive, also referred to as backdated; erasing any past mistakes showing up on your credit reports from that loan.

Forbearance

A period of time where your loans are put on pause and usually for a predetermined amount of time. You can request forbearance from federal and private student loan providers if you are going through a hardship. You will still have to pay the interest that accrues. Forbearance can also be retroactive.

I would encourage everyone to check with their student loan issuers for their qualifications and options for a deferment first as the interest will stop while you are regrouping your life and finances. Keep it in mind just because you have a deferment it does not mean you are totally off the hook; you should not be ignoring your responsibility. During the timeout you have from paying your student loans, I suggest you save your money and continue to make cut backs in your everyday spending to assure that you don't fall behind on your student loans in the future. With some dedications and vision you can tackle your responsibility to pay these obligations if you sacrifice and budget, I encourage everyone who has yet to dig a deep student loan hole to proceed with caution as this debt will not go anywhere until you pay it, so be sure when you take on this kind of obligation.

Disputing or Rehabilitation?

Just like anything else, the accuracy of student loans must also be correct if they are being reported to the credit bureaus, no matter if they are federal student loans or private. Any student loan held by a private bank, not registered with government or being serviced by the government is fair game and open to being handled like any other debt without the protection or backing of the federal government. The seven-year Statute of Limitation comes into play just as it would with any collection or charge-off account. You can employ a tactic of supplying the credit bureaus with the documentation of a deferment or a forbearance letter to show and prove that you are actually current in payments right away and possibly get the corrections on your reports as fast as 30 days. The bulk of the negativity from student loans will come from the payment history itself. It is important that you understand even if you get a student loan removed from your credit report, you are still responsible for the repayment of the loan.

Promissory Notes and Missing Paperwork

The financial industry is complicated and a lot goes on behind the scenes that we will never hear about until after the dust settles, I often advise anyone that have old private student loans to question the validity of the account itself for the lack of binding paperwork. Just like anything else, if no promissory note or contract exists; or if the paperwork goes missing, your obligation to repay these defaulted student loans do not exist. Mass produced documents by lenders and incomplete ownership records from investors can make these loans uncollectible. Don't expect for information of such to be blasted on mainstream news or delivered to your doorstep.

Chapter 11: How to Remove Mistakes from your Credit Report

Now, if you have an outstanding balance on your cards take a moment to write it down. List each card that currently has a balance, how much the balance is and how much is late. This may seem depressing when you look at the amount of debt that you have but it's important to understand. Some of the smaller debts may be possible to get rid of quickly if you're careful and you think it through. Some of the larger ones you may be able to work with pretty well at the same time.

Consider what your income is and what money you have available to spend towards your debts. Do you have enough that you could pay off a few of the smaller debts and still leave a couple of credit cards open? If you do that's great. What you want to do is call up the company and negotiate with them. Offer them a smaller amount than what is owed and tell them that if they are willing to accept that amount you can pay them immediately. Most credit card companies will jump at the offer. Even if you offer them $100 or more, less than what is actually owed, they will be perfectly happy taking the money because they know it's at least going to get them something. On the other hand, if they refuse there's no telling if you'll declare bankruptcy and then they will never get their money.

Paying off the cards will effectively close them because your credit granting company is going to take the card away from you as soon as they get their money. That's why you don't actually want to pay off all the cards that you have debt with. If you pay them all off then you're going to lose every one of them and that's going to result in no new credit being added to your credit report. That's actually going to hurt you even more than it's going to help. It may seem strange since you're looking at debt (which hurts your credit) but if you close out those accounts it's actually going to be worse than if you keep that debt hanging around at least a little while longer.

What you need to do is start making payments. Even if you owe a lot of money to a credit card company or a loan company they will rarely close the account or turn it over to a collections agency if you are making payments. They'll wait until you stop paying because, at the moment at least, they can expect to get their full amount back. If they sell the account to a collection agency they will get only a small percentage of the actual amount owed from the company. By making payments on time you increase your credit score because the algorithm that's used to calculate on time payments doesn't consider whether the actual amount due is past due. All it focuses on is whether the payment is made by the due date.

When you continue making those on time payments you also have credit. If you have credit this also counts in your favor. If you close those accounts you lose the open credit that you have and your credit score will actually go down (even though you've gotten rid of debt). So, make sure you keep those cards open and don't completely pay off the amount that's owed. Once you get the balance to a level that you can manage continue to make additional purchases and pay them. This is going to build your good credit even faster.

Once you've managed to pay the outstanding debt your credit company is less likely to pull your card away as quickly because you will still have new charges to pay off and they now have a little more trust that you're going to pay it back to them. They will likely allow you to keep the card and that's going to increase your ability to build credit. Having the open credit and then having a low minimum balance on the cards will increase your score by a lot.

What a low balance means is that you make sure

not to spend a lot of money on your credit cards and you keep the balance low. When you open credit cards you are given a limit. That's the amount of money that you are allowed to spend on that card. When you keep the balance (the amount you have spent) at the low end of this limit it actually improves your credit score. When it's high your credit score tends to go down. But you don't have to be careful about each credit card (though that's the best way to do it).

All of your credit cards are added together in order to create your total balance. So if you have three credit cards for $1,000, $1,500 and $500 your total available credit is $3,000. If your $500 credit card is completely maxed out but you haven't spent anything on the others then your credit score is still going to be pretty good because your total balance is about 16% of your available credit. On the other hand, if you had maxed out the most expensive card your credit used would be about 50% and this is not going to look so good on your credit score.

In order to improve your bad credit, it's important to pay attention to your balances. Try to keep them down and try to make payments on them frequently. This is going to help you develop a track record for trustworthiness and that's going to ensure that other credit companies are willing to give you credit and willing to let you keep that credit as well. If at all possible you want to make sure that this happens because the only way to build your credit is through having credit. Just getting rid of the debt isn't going to do enough.

Finally, if you don't have credit cards open right now you want to get them. You want to have at least three cards that have revolving credit. That means you want three credit cards that you are using and making timely payments on. If you do this, it's going to help you improve your score even as you work towards fixing some of your other problems. These new cards may have to be secured because the company does not trust your credit score and believes you will default on the money that may or may not be owed to them.

Make sure that you get the credit. Take small credit cards with secured amounts and make sure that you pay them on time. If you do this it's going to boost your score. You will definitely be surprised how quickly those positive ratings will start to show up as well. Just take advantage of them and keep building your credit. We'll explain a little more on how to get rid of some of the negative accounts in the next few chapters and how to keep your credit going strong once you've managed to fix it.

Most people who are regarded as a bad credit risk is likely to be shut out by the same society, which flourishes on credit. You may find this such a huge contradiction. Being marked as having a bad credit may result in having deep internal wounds. This is because, naturally, you would not want your neighbors to find out about your bad credit. Worse, it would be a dishonor on your part if your entire community would found out and be the topic of their gossips.

In truth, however, you do not have to deal with this type of mentality even if you have a bad credit situation. This issue is only a result of exaggeration from federal authorities and financial institutions that almost 40% to 45% of the people are in a bad credit situation. Consequently, when you are considered as a bad credit risk, the doors that were previously open would most likely be closed, which is one of the downsides of bad credit. Bad credit only implies that future financial institutions will be careful when carrying out transactions with you. For instance, you may be obliged to pay earlier than you used to, which is to be expected. Besides, if you were in the shoes of these financial institutions, you would also do the same.

If you are already in a situation of bad credit, it is best to use real money when purchasing instead of plastic, such as credit cards. This can help you spend less and you will be inclined to avoid even the most effective marketing strategies of companies. You need to get a hold of yourself by learning the techniques and tools on how you can cope with your bad credit situation. The key is to fight the situation in order to restore your good financial state as well as your dignity.

Chapter 12: How to Properly Dispute Negative Accounts

You'll be able to monitor if someone ever steals your identity and you're also going to be able to keep track of the accounts that are affecting your credit score both in positive and negative ways.

If you look at your credit report and see a lot of negative accounts, such as past due or collection accounts, consider whether they are accurate. What this means to you is that, if the negative accounts on your credit report are not 100% accurate you can request to have them removed. What you want to do is review your report and consider which accounts may not be correct. Now keep in mind you're not allowed to dispute anything that is true. Sometimes they will continue to tell you an account has been verified when you know it isn't accurate. If this happens you'll have to go above their heads and write to the original creditor, letting them know that the account is inaccurate and providing information that verifies this. This could be statements showing your bills were paid on time or letters indicating that they removed the account. Remember to send copies of these documents and not the actual letter.

Disputing false information can get a lot of accounts dropped and it can remove some of your debt because you won't have to pay for those collections or past due charges if you can prove that they are not accurate. Plus, this is going to improve your credit score and repair your credit because the negative accounts are being removed.

You could be 100% right in your disputes and the collection agency could be wrong, but for some reason you will still be met with resistance because of the structure of the credit system as a whole. Many people who have come to me with stories of them negotiating with a collection agency or a creditor not knowing the rules to the game. People have high hopes of finally getting their credit in order and they truly have good intentions, but they are met with false promises from these debt collectors who are only after their money. For some reason even after all these years; people are still under the impression that just because they pay a collection or charge-off account it will result in the derogatory item being removed from their credit, they couldn't be more wrong. No collection agency will tell you this upfront, their job isn't to help you, it is to secure a payment and collect a debt by any means necessary. If you choose not to fight, or don't have the patience, I suggest any negotiations for you to pay for a deletion should always show your agreement 100% in writing.

Write letters to the agencies with the correct but bad items you have encountered and your reasoning for which you think they should be taken off your credit report. The most important thing when writing these letters and when making any type of contact with the people at the credit report agencies is to keep communication very polite and professional. The more pleasant and prepared you are, the more you increase the chances of them helping you repair your credit. Sign and date your letters and try to write them by hand. If you have no experience with writing business letters or don't think your handwriting will be of much help, try to find templates for the type of business letter you need. The Internet is filled with appropriate templates and all you have to do is fill in information like your name and problem, without having to worry about proper business language.

The reason for which I suggested you send your letter with the additional costs of certified mail is that so you know exactly when your letter has reached its destination. It is extremely important to be aware of this, because the law stipulates that the agencies have to verify whatever claims you make and respond to you after a reasonable time of usually thirty days. This law is well known by everyone working in credit report agencies, which is why they will proceed to check your credit report immediately because if not, the item you contested becomes unverifiable and will be removed by default. If you see the customary period of time has passed, write another letter reminding the agency to remove the contested entry, in accordance with the law.

Don't cram all the problems you've encountered into a single letter, as that will unnecessarily encumber the employee working on fixing your credit reports and if they are stressed a decision in your favor will be harder to reach. Keep it about two or three issues per letter and, if you think you are concise and specific in your requests, maybe add a few more. It all really depends on what the problems you've encountered contain and how you have formulated your reasoning. If you send a letter and it has a huge number of problems you've considered wrong, they might categorize your claims as frivolous. The law permits credit reporting agencies to discard "frivolous requests" so be careful how many issues per letter you dispute and how you express yourself in your letter. Just state who you are and what you think the problem is, that you have a right to have your claims investigated and that you are happy to help the agency with all the information they require. Professionalism and politeness will go a long way. If you think it will be best to send more letters, try to send them a few days apart from each other, so that the people working at the agency have more time to investigate each claim in an adequate way.

After you send your first letter, the process of reviewing your credit report begins. As you probably know, the negative information you've submitted may actually be accurate and the reply to your letter might say that they've investigated your claim and they can't remove the item from your credit report. If you want to keep pressing the issue, write a second letter including all the information from the letter and request further verifications as well as the contact information of the employees that were responsible at the creditor company. Usually they will have no problem with giving you the contact information of the person at the creditor firm, so now you can discuss directly with them about the problem and possibly begin a negotiation on the matter.

If you've cleared some issues from your credit report, you can consider the first steps towards repairing your credit to be successful. Chances are that, after correcting some errors and trying to get the problems removed by default or re-evaluated, you'll still be left with problems. These are the most difficult to remove as they are accurate and legitimate fiscal missteps that you've taken at one point. This is why you should directly contact the person at the creditor office, as these kinds of problems can only be removed from your credit report through extensive negotiations, which will now begin.

Even if you know that you can repair your credit, don't just jump into it without coming up with a strategy. The first thing you should do is to list all the accounts you intend to dispute then follow with sending dispute letters for each of the accounts. You can use any of the three methods:

- Send the dispute letters through email

- Visit the individual credit bureau's office then file the dispute

- File the dispute online

Don't aim to have zero balances for accounts that you settle. Instead, you should have them removed completely because a zero balance taints your rating. This zero balance will show in your report for 7 years or more; it speaks that creditors should take caution when dealing with you. You don't want that! You would rather fail to pay the debt to let it expire instead of having your credit score tainted by the derogatory zero balance! As such, even if you are to go into a pay to delete arrangement with a creditor. So, what should you have in your dispute letters?

- Your Last and First name (must be spelled correctly)

- Your SSN

- Your Driver's license

- Your current home address

- Your W2 form or pay stub showing your name and SSN

- Your first and last name spelled accurately

- Any other forms of identification you may have

If you don't correct all these mistakes your dispute will not be accepted, it's also important to note that all the necessary information in the dispute. Look out for variations in account numbers for the same account as creditors could sometimes have different numbers for different bureaus.

Chapter 13: The Right Mindset

Many folks suffer a financial crisis at some point. They may have to deal with overspending, loss of a job, a family member or personal illness. These financial problems can be and usually are, overwhelming. To make these situations worse, most people don't even know where to begin to solve these financial dilemmas. Our goal here is to shine some light on the strategies to help get youth Accumulating basic consumer debt will chain you into slavery and you could possibly spend your life held down by your own obligations to repay these loans. Who do you work for? I don't care what you say; the real answer is your creditors if you are currently stuck paying debt. There are many forms of "dumb debt" you can get trapped into. We are all sold images and lifestyles hundreds of times per day to provoke this materialistic behavior.

The person or institution lending you the money is trusting that you have the ability to hold up your end of the bargain, basically. Sometimes, it may seem impossible to live your life without the option to get a credit, but this is what bad credit eventually leads to. Since your ability to repay a loan has been affected, either by the inability to pay or a series of misunderstandings, other lenders will become skeptical when it comes to granting you a new credit.

But how do you get a credit in the first place? What is the process you have to go through to loan money? Well, it all starts with a credit application to a bank or some other party that has the necessary finances. Your application is reviewed and, if they think there won't be a problem with getting their money back, you sign a contract and get your money in no time. This application contains a large amount of relevant information about yourself such as your employment situation, your monthly income and other credits or obligations like rent, for instance. The application you submit to a lender is used to obtain a credit report from one or several reporting agencies, depending on how much money you need. These two documents are given scores and, if your score is enough you'll get the money you need. If not, your application will be rejected. If you don't fall into any of these categories, then a judgment call has to be made by the person or institution providing the credit. The more "good credit" criteria you meet, the more likely it is that you will get your credit.

However, there are several things that you must consider before you put yourself into the category of citizens unaffected by bad credit. First of all, the lenders look for certain things in your application, such as an up to date credit report and no late payments on your other financial obligations. They are interested to see if you've had a job for more than a year and have a stable income, as well as a stable residence. They also evaluate the situation of your utility and phone bills and appreciate if you include information about additional credit cards or other types of cards. It is not only banks and money lenders that look at this type of information. Sometimes, if you want to get a new job, your employer will conduct this type of research too, so maintaining a good credit is crucial in these troubled times we live in.

What type of credit should you get? That depends on what you plan to do with the money. The most used types of credit are secured and signature credits. For smaller loans, there's no need for that, as no institution would like to end up with a store of household items, so they lend you money or issue a credit card in your name simply based on the strength of your credit so far.

There is hope; you as the borrower have many options to get rid of debt. You can take advantage of budgeting and other techniques, such as debt consolidation, debt settlement, credit counseling, and bankruptcy procedures. You just have to choose the best strategy that will work for you. When choosing from the various options, you have to consider your debt level, your discipline, and plans for the future.

The Good Debt

Some people find it hard to live debt free at least they will have some debt to pay off. While some debts are discouraged, good debt is considered as the money you borrow so that you can pay for things that you really need or things that increase in value. On the flip side, bad debt is one that arises from things that you only want and often decrease in value.

Of course, debt isn't a bad thing; it's just how you use the money that matters.

For a good debt, you will always have a good reason to justify it, and a developed plan for paying it so that you can clear the debt as quickly as possible.

An individual with good debt will also have the cheapest methods of borrowing money. They will do this by looking at the borrowing method, rate of interest, credit amount, and charges that are appropriate to them.

Sometimes, it may imply a deal with the least possible interest rate, but sometimes, it may not.

Examples of good debt

Paying for medical care. There is no fixed amount of money to borrow to ensure your loved one stays healthy. You can manage to pay off the money you borrow, but it is impossible to replace a human life. If a person requires expensive treatments to ensure they remain healthy, this would be an acceptable debt, no matter what.

Borrow money for education. When you apply for a student loan debt, you aren't making a wrong decision. In general, people with college degrees earn more income in their life than those without a degree.

And applying for a student loan so that you can support the education of your child defeats the idea of using your savings. After all, you cannot borrow money to pay for your savings. Multiple government programs provide low-interest student loans, and you can always cut student loan interest on your taxes.

Taking out a mortgage on a home. Taking a loan of this amount can be overwhelming, but purchasing a house creates ownership in something that will house you, and generate some retirement money. Even while you struggle to clear your debt, you may consider it an advantage to put any available liquid cash as a deposit, though it may not be the right choice.

A home mortgage interest is cut on your taxes, and the rate of interest is lower on your home loan than on the credit card. In other words, it is important to have money to pay for other expenses instead of credit.

Though purchasing a house was initially considered a strong, future-proof investment, certain homeowners do find themselves on the wrong side on their home mortgage loan. They owe banks more than the value of their homes. However, strategic planning, purchasing only what you can afford, and maintaining low interest by having good credit may allow you to purchase a home that one day you will own completely.

Buying a car. If you don't have public transport in your area, or you cannot manage to get someone with whom you can carpool with, then you may have to consider buying a car. An auto loan can either be "good" or "bad", but the main thing is to ensure that the auto loan is a good debt, so look for the lowest possible rates on your loan. In addition, you need to make a large down payment while ensuring that you remain with some cash on hand just in case you need it.

Your best goal should be to go for a used car model instead of a brand-new one, possibly saving yourself thousands on the sticker price and the interest that is paid throughout the loan.

Business loans. While this may not be seen as good debt, borrowing money to begin a business or expand a business is perhaps a great idea if the business is thriving. After all, you need money to make more money, right?

Sometimes, you may have to borrow capital to employ new people, purchase a new device, pay for advertisement, or even develop the first new widget you designed. The point is that you borrow this money to expand the business or increase income, then this will count as good debt.

What is Bad Debt?

Bad debt is that which depletes your wealth and isn't affordable. Plus, it provides no means to pay for itself.

Bad debts may have no realistic repayment plans and usually deplete when people buy things at an impulse. If you aren't sure whether you can repay the money, then don't borrow the money because that will be a bad debt.

Examples of bad debt

The credit card debt. A typical household in the United States has a balance of more than $10,000 on their credit card every month. However, the debt usually increases faster than we may realize and is always used to purchase things that we want instead of need. It is easier to think that you can afford something using a card than paying it with cash.

Borrowing from a 401K. When you ask for money from a 401K program, you will need to chat with the IRS, and if you aren't using the money to purchase a home, you will need to pay the loan in five years. If you fail to pay it back, you risk being charged with a severe penalty. Also, the interest that you pay on the loan will get taxed twice.

You can't get a loan to fund your retirement. For that reason, borrowing money from your retirement plan to use it to pay for anything that isn't part of retirement is a bad idea. You will be putting your retirement at risk when you get a loan from a 401k, so don't make this mistake.

Payday loans. It may appear easy to borrow money from payday loan firms, but it is hard to pay it back. These companies offer loans with very high interest rates. The companies take advantage of the fact that many people need that money. As a result, borrowing a small amount may end up costing you a lot.

Payday loans aren't considered the worst kind of debt that you can take on. If you really need a short-term loan, it is better to go for a cash advance on a credit card rather than borrow money from these firms.

Using consolidation or settlement strategies to pay down debts

Debt consolidation is another strategy that can be used to manage your debts. It involves combining two or more debts at a lower interest rate than you are currently at.

But, it is worth doing your research and making some phone calls to see if there is a company that's willing to work with you. If you can lower your monthly bill to a manageable level, at an interest rate that's reasonable, that can make all the difference in handling your debt.

Like many strategies, you have had the option of

settling your debts with companies for decades. Lenders always want as much money as you can give them versus being shafted for the entire amount in a bankruptcy. It is just that consolidation and settlement options rose in popularity during the recent financial crisis making it appear in more articles and news pieces than ever before.

If you have savings to pay off your debts, then start with the most expensive. Otherwise, utilize settlement options where you are able to reduce the amount owed if you pay a certain amount right now. As long as the account shows paid in full, with a strong payment history, your scores are going to increase. It doesn't matter if you needed to use debt settlement strategies to make the debt end. It just matters that you have paid the debt off instead of letting it go into arrears.

Negotiate with Credit Companies

Another thing not a lot of people know is that you can negotiate with credit companies. So you're able to take the collection letter they send you or a past due notice that has been sent to you and discuss it with them. In many cases they will take a lower amount than what's on the bill just so that they can guarantee they'll get something

Let's say you owe Discover $1,000. They really want to get their money so they send you a past due notice. But for several months you've ignored that past due notice and now they've sent it to collections. The collections agency may offer you a settlement. Maybe they say they'll take $900 if you just pay it to them right then and there. You have the opportunity to call them and request that they take a lesser amount.

If you talk to the collection agency and they agree to take a lesser amount you will have to send that payment in full. Make sure that when you send them the check you write out the words 'paid in full' on the check. Make a copy of the check for your own records as well. Once they cash that check your account is legally considered to be paid in full and they are no longer able to come after you for more money.

Cut the Credit Cards

If you're looking to save some money, then you need to make sure you're spending less. That means getting rid of all those credit cards. If you're able to avoid the temptation to purchase things you can put one credit card in the back of your purse or wallet. Choose a card that will work anywhere such as a major credit card company.

This is for emergencies only. An emergency doesn't mean you found something that you really want to have. It means that your car broke down and needs to be towed, or you run out of gas.

The rest of the credit cards you decide to keep should be locked up somewhere in your home. Put them in a safe or lockbox. This way you have to actively think about getting the card out again before you're able to actually use it. This will keep you from using the card in a spur of the moment fashion and will ensure that you still have it available if absolutely necessary.

The best thing to do is make one to two small purchases on your credit card every few months. Try to space out using different cards so that none of them get taken but you don't owe very much money each month. You want to keep the amount negligible. That means it is low enough that it really doesn't affect your overall budget. This is going to let you keep the card but, at the same time, it's not going to completely break the bank.

Talking to Creditors

Tell them the reason why you're having a difficult time paying the debts. Most companies will negotiate a modified payment plan so monthly payments become more manageable. If you wait for the accounts to go into default, it can and most likely will affect your credit score negatively, which is what we're looking to avoid. Once in default, the collector will start calling.

Taking Advantage of Debt Relief Services

A debt settlement company will put your deposits in a bank account, which is managed by a **3rd**-party. Although you own the funds and accrued interests, the account manager will charge a fee for services because they'll be the one to transfer funds from your account to the creditors' accounts. Before signing up for a debt relief service, you must know the exact price and terms that the company offers. You also need to know how long it will be before you can expect to get results. The debt relief service firm must also inform you how much the negotiated debt is and the amount of money need to have in the designated bank account before the company can tender an offer to each of the creditors. In addition, they must inform you about the probable consequences if you fail to make the payments.

There are cases when creditors report settled

debts to the Internal Revenue Service. Unless you are insolvent, the IRS may consider savings from debt relief service as taxable; meaning they may consider the situation as an income generation. As such, it is best for them to talk to an accountant. We don't want the IRS after us when we just got rid of the calls from the collection agency!

It may sound like all the debt relief companies are out to scam us, they're not. We, the consumer, just need to be aware of all the steps involved in order to make an informed choice about whether or not this particular option is right for our situation.

Ideally you want a company with a positive Better Business Bureau rating. You must know how much each service will cost and how long you'll have to wait to get the expected results. It is important to read any contract you enter into thoroughly and get every promise in writing.

Credit Counseling

Credit counseling is a service offered by some organizations to borrowers seeking advice on how they can manage their finances. It usually includes budgeting, workshops and educational resources. A counselor must receive training and certification in budgeting, money and debt management, and consumer credit. He or she must be able to tackle your financial situation and offer help in creating a personalized plan. Usually, the first session can last for an hour or more.

Debt Management Plan

If you can no longer pay your debts or like me, just have a lot of debt already, a credit counselor will suggest that we take advantage of a debt management plan. However, this plan is not an exact fit for everyone. In a debt management plan, you deposit your money monthly to the credit counseling organization, which in turn, pays the debts on your behalf. The credit counselor negotiates with the creditors and drafts a payment schedule. Creditors may be amenable to waive some fees or reduce interest rates. Usually, a debt management plan takes about 4 years to be completed, depending on your amount of debt. If you want to take advantage of this type of plan, make sure to talk with the credit counselor about the monthly payments, length of time to pay off the debts and any other concerns you may have. This is a great option for someone who would like to be "hands off" while repaying their debt and repairing their credit.

Debt Settlement Program

A debt settlement program can be risky, so you have to consider some factors before taking advantage of it. Many of these programs require that you deposit money on an account for at least 3 years before the debt settlement company can settle your debts. Many people are unsuccessful with this plan because they fail to deposit money into the account. As such, it is important for the borrower (you) to have a budget and stick to it so that you have enough money for the monthly payments. Although it seems simple this act is lost on many folks, keeping them stuck in the debt cycle.

Another aspect to consider is that some creditors will not negotiate for a debt settlement; therefore, the debt settlement company may not be able to pay some of your debts. In addition, some of these debt settlement companies pay off smaller debts first, leaving the large debts to continue growing.

Lastly, the debt settlement company will suggest that you stop paying your creditors. This decision will result in a significant drop to your credit score. The debts will also incur fees and penalties for nonpayment. In addition, you could continue to get calls from debt collectors and creditors, or face court cases for your decision to refuse paying off your debt.

A debt settlement program is only as good as the debt settlement company that offers it. Many do deliver on their promises, and some even provide guarantees that they can get rid of as much as 60% of the original debt. These firms may also collect hefty fees before the debts are settled, though the government prohibits these practices.

Chapter 14: Handling Foreclosure

Maybe you've lost your job or are experiencing some other financial dilemma. Maybe you had a fixed interest rate for a few years but then had to pay higher monthly installments because the interest rate made a significant jump. Mortgage anxiety is a problem of many people. It's good to know that there are many ways to avoid foreclosures.

What to Do if a Person Can't Pay Monthly Payments on Time

If you have difficulty paying the monthly amount in a hybrid adjustable rate mortgage, you can refinance the mortgage with a fixed rate loan. It is always advisable to read the loan contract carefully and check the prepayment penalty provisions. Many of these loans often charge high prepayment penalties so that you will be discouraged from paying off the mortgage early. It may not be good to avail of fixed-rate refinancing if you plan to sell your home right after the approval of a refinanced loan. It's best to call the representative from the mortgage company as soon as possible if you have difficulty in making the monthly payments. In addition, you can also qualify for the program if you were approved for your mortgage prior to 2009; the monthly payment on your original loan was at least 31% of present gross income and you're currently experiencing financial hardship.

How to Negotiate with the Creditor

You must be prepared with all of your appropriate documents and financial information before you call your lender. Failure to do this will result in a loss of trust between you and the person you speak with. This little bit of preparation can go a long way. You really want to have a solid grasp on whether the financial problem is a permanent or temporary one so that you can negotiate and reason with your lender. You must be decisive in what you want to do with your mortgage.

You'll want to make note of the dates and times, the name of the representative you spoke with, the nature of the conversation, as well as the result of the communication. If you make an oral request (on the phone), you must ensure that you follow that with a written request. During the negotiation process, you must continue to live in your home in order to qualify for assistance. If you rent out your property, your creditor will not approve the request because the home is no longer your primary residence.

During the foreclosure prevention procedure, it's beneficial to seek counseling from a reputable housing counseling organization to help you get through the whole process with ease. If you do use a counseling service, be careful about counselors who guarantee non-foreclosure of your home, or firms that charge significant upfront fees.

Avoiding Predatory Scams

A scammer can prepare pitches to lure homeowners, who have problems paying off their mortgage. He can present himself as a foreclosure prevention specialist, who will charge significant fees for paper work or phone calls. He will give you false hope when you're at your most desperate, prompting you to share your personal information. In the end, you've been taken advantage of and still have to pay your mortgage.

One scam used is to encourage homeowners to take advantage of a lease/buy back scheme. The scammer will ask you to sign a deed with a guarantee that you'll be able to buy back your house while you rent it. This scheme will eventually get you evicted from your own home while the scammer gets the home equity.

Lastly, you can be a victim of a bait-and-switch fraud. The scammer will ask you to sign documents with a promise to keep your current loan. You fail to recognize that you're signing a deed to your home, and only realize once an eviction notice is delivered.

As noted before, you must do your homework and research on any person or company you decide to work with. A simple Google search is a great way to start. You can also ask your friends and family if they are familiar with the person in question. A little bit of work can save you a ton of trouble and stress.

Chapter 15: Mistakes to Avoid while Repairing your Credit

Hurting your score will affect your life. Your credit score could either make or break your finances, so it is very important to know what ruins a good score.

Your credit score is very much important to the moneylending industry. This helps businesses, organizations, and creditors to determine risky credit card users.

Keeping track of your credit digits isn't enough. Being aware of the common mistakes is what matters. Know the destructive points in your score, and avoid committing credit mistakes.

Here are the common mistakes you need to avoid:

Late payments

Always make sure to pay on the scheduled date.

Missed payments

Stay updated with your credit transactions. Don't miss the date for paying your bills. Missing payments is a big credit misstep.

Avoid forgetting due dates. If you tend to be forgetful, set up electronic reminders, or mark your calendars for the date of payment.

Not paying the accurate amount due

If you don't pay the right amount of credit you owe the bank or credit card company will report your record. This will cost you higher interest rates. Make it a habit to budget your expenses wisely. Save the allotted money needed and pay the right amount due.

Owning Multiple Accounts

Having different kinds of cards may be alluring with the best offers, deals, gifts, and discounts it brings. It is very hard to resist signing up for a new card. But the lending industry might think you're a desperate card holder. Moneylenders may worry that you're dealing with monetary problems. Creditors may indicate that you're drowning in your debts.

Avoid credit card inquiries. Avoid holding multiple credit accounts. Reaching the "maxed out" limit

Maxing out your credit card is a bad sign. Owing to a high amount of debt is not good. This will hurt your debit and credit ratio.

Avoid overusing and misusing your card. Instead, use your credit card in moderation. Keep your credit usage from 10-30% only.

Not notifying your creditors for slight changes

Notify your creditors about changes of data. Make it a point to update your creditors about slight changes: your residential address, signature updates, etc. Using an incomplete and/or illegal name in financial papers

Do not write your name incomplete. This will be a conflict on summing up your credit score.

Avoid using your nickname when filling out financial papers, as this will cause complications for banks and credit card companies in summing up your score. Make sure to write your complete name and write legibly to avoid confusion.

Chapter 16: How to NOT Obsess on a High Credit Score

High score in your credit card? It's very unusual but some people aim for it - That perfect credit score of 850. Some people will do anything to reach that.

The pursuit to perfect your credit score may lead to obsession. What matters most to you now is aiming for that high score. Just live your life as it is and let your finances flow naturally. Stop obsessing of reaching that high credit score. To get the best rates and deals there's no need to aim for that 850. All it takes is a score that shows you are creditworthy, so do not get obsessed. To control your obsession on achieving that high score, here are some helpful tips:

Live normally, financially

Live your everyday life as it is. No need to use your credit card on all your expenses. If you bring enough money with you, don't use your credit card. With the intent of keeping up a sophisticated lifestyle, you're not using your credit card responsibly.

126

Stop the swiping spree

Avoid using your credit card on a swiping spree. Stop overusing and/or misusing your credit card. Using your credit to purchase barely anything is unhealthy. Moneylenders may mistake your identity as credit card dependent, so it's better to refrain yourself from this kind of habit. Balance the utilization of your credit card versus the money you're bringing.

Avoid checking your credit report more often

Avoid frequently checking your credit reports. Credit card records are not perfectly accurate. According to the 2013 Federal Trade Commission, 25% of credit card reports contain inaccuracies. Almost all credit reports have errors, so do not stress if you only get 780.

A perfect credit score is not a requirement

Let me tell you this: a perfect credit score is not required. Remember, a credit score of 720 is enough for a good score. The best scores for benefits, deals, and low rates aren't the highest ones. In fact, these credit scores range between 720 and 780, so don't stress if you didn't reach

800+. Credit scores that range from 780-850 barely make a difference. You will only get your bank or credit card company's respect. There is no world record to beat for that. You won't get recognized if you have a perfect credit score.

If change is constant, so is your credit score

Able to reach that 850 credit score? It won't remain for too long. Due to many factors, scores constantly change. High credit scores are not permanent, so stop minding the increases and decreases of those three digits.

Chapter 17: Getting Late Payments Deleted like the Pros

You can actually ask credit card companies to get rid of problems on your credit report even if you are actually in the wrong. What you want to do is simply call or write to the credit card company directly. Let them know that you understand you were late on a payment but point out your history and show that you have not been late in the past and you made a one-time mistake. (If you have been late frequently they probably won't work with you as much.).

Now if you have never made this mistake before or if you have rarely done it the credit card company may be willing to wave a late payment. This would mean that they take the late payment remark from your history and you may not even have to pay a fine. But by taking off the mark on your history they are improving your credit score. That one little late payment can be a big problem and it can result in your score taking a big hit. If it gets removed you no longer have to worry about it and your credit score could go up quite a bit.

What this means is you could have a long history

of late payments with your oldest account but you're getting more positive marks on your credit from that account being so old than you are negative marks for the late payments. You don't ever want to close your oldest account unless you have no way around it. This account is doing great things for you.

Now if you have multiple accounts that are very close to the same age and one has a lot of negative marks you can close it. What you don't want to do is close the only account you have that's older than two years. (Of course, the older the account is the better it is for you.) Only close this account if there's an important reason for it or if you have another account that is very close to the same age and is giving you the same benefits when it comes to account history.

All those 'free quote' websites are actually hurting your credit score as well. You need to make sure that you are not signing up for a lot of those quotes. Even when you're searching for something like car insurance or health insurance you need to be careful. Free quotes may sound great but how do you think they're able to give you that quote? They need to know a little more about you in order to give you something that they can guarantee and that means they run your credit history and check out your credit score. That helps them to know whether you'll pay your bills or not and that affects your quote.

Now you may be thinking, I pay it off every month so how could I be hurting my credit score? Well, when your bank or credit union sends you a bill they are telling you how much money you owe. That amount is also being sent to the credit reporting agency, which uses it to calculate your credit utilization rate. If your balance is $500 and you owe $500 then your utilization rate is 100% and that's going to look really bad on your credit report. It's going to lower your score by quite a bit.

If you have a bad credit history, or it's in a state which you don't want it to be, you aren't alone. Improving your credit score takes time, but the earlier you begin to fix the issues that may be slowing it down, the faster your credit score will rise.

Keeping a close check on your credit enables you to understand the way your financial actions impact your credit. This will also help you to respond to any immediate change in your score and know when you have attained excellent credit, and you may qualify for better interest credit card offers. Alternatively, learning how your credit score changes over time gives you the ability to manage your financial wellbeing. However, it is vital to ensure that you monitor your credit score without damaging it.

Hard and Soft Inquiries

Credit requests, or inquiries about your credit report information, are categorized under soft and hard inquiries. A soft inquiry refers to any inquiry where a prospective lender isn't reviewing your credit. On the other hand, a hard credit request is when your credit is getting reviewed because you have applied for credit using a prospective lender. Hard inquiries consist of a sizable amount of your general credit score and tend to have the least, short-term effect. However, if you have many of them in the short term, it may indicate that you are a risky borrower. This may lead to a lower credit score.

That is the reason the time to begin fixing your credit is now—before the time comes where you really need it. Luckily, it is not that hard to improve your credit score. Below are some easy processes that you can implement:

Make a Humble Request

Say you attempted to remove the derogatory comment, account marked "Paid as agreed", but failed. Should you now give up? Or give it another try?

Don't give up; you can instead make a humble

request or even ask interestingly.

Creditors have the authority to allow credit bureaus to eliminate records from your credit report at any time. So when all else doesn't work, call and make a humble request. You will be surprised to learn how a humble request may assist you.

Increase the limits of your credit

One method that you can use to ensure that you have a good ratio is to clear your balances, but another method is to increase the limit of your credit.

To have the limit/s increased, you need to call and ask politely. If you have a good payment history, most credit card companies are going to be happy to increase your limit.

Even as they increase your limit, remain disciplined so that you don't use extra available credit—if you do so, you will return to the original credit ratio boat. And you will be in big debt.

Open a new credit card account

You can also positively increase your credit score by choosing to open a new account. Your only goal is to make sure that there is no balance on this card, and the credit available will possibly rise depending on the limit.

Get a card that doesn't require you to pay an annual fee. Your best route has to be through a bank—of which you already have a bank account with. The cards that don't have a yearly charge tend to demand high-interest rates, but if you don't leave a balance, this may not affect you.

However, again, you need to be smart. Your target shouldn't be to have more cash but to improve the credit score. If you think you may easily use the balance on the new account, then it is better that you don't open another one.

Understanding and boosting your credit score

Your credit health determines your financial future. In other words, when you have strong credit health, you get access to loans with a low-interest rate, and this will save you a lot of bucks in the long term. On the other hand, a bad credit score may limit your chances of getting funds to buy a vehicle, or get the best rates for a credit card.

The credit sector can be complicated, and even

challenging to start. The first step to get a strong credit score begins with learning everything about your credit score. By mastering your credit score and the things to do to change it, you will crack your credit potential and realize your goals.

A credit score has three numbers that reveal much about your credit report, and lenders depend on this to define the health of your credit. An algorithm determines the scores of a credit. This algorithm relies on information from your credit report. Credit scores were developed to show the probabilities that you can achieve in your payment agreement.

There is a misconception that each is allocated a single credit score, which is accessed by lenders and bureaus. This is a lie because you can have multiple credit scores. And the reason is that there are many credit agencies, and different strategies to use to calculate information, and credit scores at different times. If you aren't aware, there are more than a hundred models of scoring, but the most popular models comprise of VantageScore and FICOScore.

Don't be scared about monitoring every credit score, but keep a close eye on the popular scores, which many lenders use to determine whether you qualify for a credit or not.

A credit report, as the name suggests, contains data and information that credit agencies get from lenders. In the United States, numerous credit agencies process a consumer's credit report. But the main credit agencies that most businesses and financial organizations use include TransUnion, Equifax, and Experian.

Credit Card Usage

Your credit usage is also called "debt-to-limit ratio". This ratio determines the size of your whole credit card limit. An ethical principle to follow is to ensure that your credit use ratio doesn't go past 30%. This means the lower the credit card usage, the better. When you have a higher credit card usage ratio, it will reduce your credit score and may cause prospective lenders to become scared that you may not manage more debt.

There are different methods used to reduce the credit use ratio—right from paying a debt to raising the limit on the credit.

Timing is everything

The older the accounts, the better they are for everyone, as your primary credit accounts are aging, you should be learning. You can get in position to help your family build credit or start your own community of credit for investment purposes without having to ask others for help. How powerful can you be when your whole family has perfect credit?

Typically, unless you get added as an Authorized user from a family member or a friend, people will want to charge you as the strategy of piggybacking on other people's positive credit accounts has become well known. It's pretty standard for people to pay to be added to positive aged trade lines, companies exist and thrive on brokering these positive accounts to clients who need a boost in credit for funding purposes. This practice is 100% legal. The primary account holder can add authorized users by simply calling their credit card companies.

Chapter 18: Managing Your Personal Finances in a Stress-Free Way

The Importance of Money Management

Do you find yourself with different credit cards, a mortgage, and an auto loan?

There are methods to help you make this manageable. It takes time to discover the ins and outs of it and twist your budget so that it can satisfy your needs:

You know where your money is going

This is a huge benefit since it will allow you to watch the way you spend money and save more. You can track your spending for several months and then balance the budget to assign a lot of money to savings, or even retirement.

If you handle your money well, you will manage to make early payments, and avoid surpassing the limit on the credit card.

When you stick to your budget, these methods will assist you to save money.

This prevents you from spending much money.

A better plan of retirement

When you save now and manage your money in the right way, it will benefit you in the long term. First, it will force you to look into the future and look into your retirement plans.

When you implement your money management skills, you will be building yourself a strong retirement plan. The money that you save and invest will grow as time goes by.

Allows you to concentrate on your goals

You will avoid unnecessary expenditure that doesn't support achieving financial goals. If you are dealing with limited resources, budgeting makes it complex to fulfill your ends.

You organize your spending and savings

When you divide your income into different types of expenditure and savings, a budget will allow you to remain aware of the type of expenditure that drains the portion of your money. This way, it is simple for you to set adjustments. Good money management acts as a reference for organizing receipts, bills, and financial statements. Once you organize all your financial transactions, you will save effort and time.

You can speak to your partner about money

If you do share your income with your spouse, then a budget can be the best tool to show how money is spent. This increases teamwork to work on a common financial target and prevents arguments on the way money is used. Creating a budget together with your spouse will help you to avoid conflict and eliminate personal conflicts on the way money is spent.

It determines whether you can take on debt and how much

Taking on debt isn't a bad thing, but it is important, especially if you cannot afford it. A budget will indicate the amount of debt load you can take on without getting stressed.

Budgeting

When you budget, you get the chance to single

out and eliminate unnecessary spendings such as on penalties, late fees, and interests. These little savings can increase with time.

A budget refers to a plan that takes into account your monthly cash flow and outflow. This is a snapshot of what you own, and what you expect to spend, and which will allow you to realize your financial goals by assisting you in highlighting your saving and spending.

Creating a budget is the most crucial aspect of financial planning. The amount of money you have doesn't indicate how much money you make, but instead, it is how effective your budgeting is. If you want to take care of your finances, then you will have to understand where your money is flowing to. Contrary to popular belief that budgeting is hard, it isn't, and it doesn't eliminate the fun from your life. A budget will save you from an unexpected financial crisis and a life of debt.

Monitor your expenses and income

The first thing to building a budget is to determine the amount of money you have and what you are spending it on. By monitoring your expenses, you will manage to classify how you spend your money. Planning how you spend your money is critical because you can tell how much you want to spend in every category. You can monitor your income and expenses by creating a journal, spreadsheet, or cash book. Every time you make money, you can monitor it as income, and every time you spend money, you can track it as an expense.

If you use a debit card, try to track back three months of your spending to get a comprehensive picture of your expenditure.

Evaluate your income

The next stage is to assess your income. You can do this by computing the amount of income you get via gifts, scholarships, *etc*.

Determine your expenses

Once you know your monthly income, next is to determine the total of your expenses. First, you need to define what your fixed, variable expenses are. Fixed expenses, sales, and bills have the same price every month. The fixed expenses comprise of car payments, internet, and rent. Variable expenses refer to costs that change, such as utilities and groceries.

Be sure to include payments of debt in your budget. Find out the amount that you can contribute towards your debts to make sure that you are on the correct path to financial stability. Handling debts and savings go hand in hand.

Building a Saving Strategy

It is quite easy to forget to save money. Keep in mind that you always pay yourself first. Give it a try using 10-20% of your income savings. Since savings increase, you can choose to include money that you didn't spend in the budget to save.

Many people know how to manage the little money they get when the month ends, but they find it hard to save when they have a tight budget. If you look at finance articles online, you will see different types of saving methods—right from freezing all spending to packing your own lunch for a month. But how can you determine which one's work? In this section, you will learn easy money-saving strategies you can implement and how you can make them work for you:

Stay out of debt

Being debt free will help you to save cash; if you

can pay off all your debt, you will get the chance to organize your debt.

The stats on eliminating debt can be shocking. For example, the Claris poll showed that only 22% of people attempted this strategy, and 26% reported that it worked for them. In other words, this strategy can help you save money.

Staying out of debt can save you a good sum of cash, but many people find it hard to pay off their debts.

Be a Minimalist

Adopting a minimalist approach is a type of voluntary simplicity. It requires a person to cut down on costs so that they concentrate on what is important. A minimalist's life generally means owning a smaller house, fewer "toys", and fewer clothes. But it also implies minimal work and more time to do the things that you like.

This is a great saving strategy that works even for those who don't want to use it. A minimalist approach can be the effect of other methods to save. In most cases, many people scaled their life to stick to their budget. Then, with time, they discovered that their simple lifestyle helped them save more.

There are various misconceptions about minimalism. A blog about minimalism jokes that minimalists live in small apartments and don't have jobs, cars, TVs, or more than 100 objects.

The purpose of minimalism is to free yourself from issues in life that aren't important. It is not focused on sacrifice; it merely involves eliminating things that you don't want to have in life or creating room for things that you care about. As a result, living with fewer items can make you feel satisfied.

If you aren't sure whether you can deal with this kind of life, you can start small and slowly identify a few things in your life that you don't want. For example, if your wardrobe is filled with many things, perhaps throw out or donate some clothes. Or if you spend a lot of time online, plan to reduce your screen time.

Whatever you decide to do, make sure that you don't simplify your life by surrendering on the things you value or treasure; instead, choose things that require the most work for the least reward.

If you are searching for methods to help you save a lot of money, these methods are the best ones to begin with. Since they have worked for other people, there is a big chance that they will work for you too. However, make sure that you don't jump in and try all the methods at once—just select strategies that you believe may work for you.

Investing your Money

Investing your money gives you a chance to grow your money, and even make more than what you have. However, not everyone who decides to invest their money makes profits; some have lost tons of money in the process. There is a different way to invest your money, and this section will introduce you to some of the most common strategies for investment:

Online investing can be a quick and convenient method that is more affordable than other methods. But before you can handle your online investment, you need to ask yourself several questions:

Online investing is designed for everyone. By choosing this option, you hold the responsibility to research all investments and make all investment decisions regarding your online account. If you don't feel okay as that kind of investor, you could be comfortable working with a financial advisor. If you like to manage your investment portfolio and feel secure that you have enough knowledge, you may decide to go with online investment.

Stop Spending

If you can't stop spending money that you don't have, this book will only temporarily fix your problems, if it is even able to do that. If you have a habit of living out of your means and buying things you cannot afford, this is your chance to fix that. If you want to fix your credit and improve your life financially, you must take care of these things. So sit tight, make a budget, and find something that works, and cut up those maxed out credit cards if you have to.

Chapter 19: How to Handle Medical Collections

The last thing you should know about is how to settle medical debts. It is unfortunate, but in the United States, we often have to contend with high medical costs and a confusing system that can cripple us financially for years after an illness or accident. Even with insurance, there are co-pays, deductibles, and procedures that fall outside of some plans coverage. Even if you are not currently contending with medical debts, it is a good thing to understand in case they hit your family.

When you start on your journey to understand and settle your medical debts, it is important to understand that the system was not made for consumer usability. It will be a hard and tedious job that will require a lot of time, energy, and patience to complete. You will need to keep everything you receive in an organized file and pay attention to things like deadlines and necessary procedures to be successful. That being said, it can be done, even without professional help.

The worst thing you could do when faced with

medical debt is to ignore it, so make sure to start as soon as you are able. In most cases, you must attempt to negotiate your bills within the first 90 days of incurring the debt, otherwise, it can be sent to a collection agency, which will be explained later.

The very first thing you need to do is organize your bills. You will not receive a single bill from your hospital. You can also get billed by an ambulance company, labs, and pharmacy. Gather all of these into a file and review them to understand what you need to do. Write down the contact information for each of the services you are being billed for, what you were charged for, and how much you owe for each thing. It is a good idea to put this all into a spreadsheet.

Using the information you gathered from the bills, look for billing discrepancies. If you find anything like the things listed here in your bills you can get them removed. Some things to look for are:

Being billed for a full day's stay when you did not stay the full day such as on the day you are admitted or released

Being billed for any items like gowns, gloves, or sheets that should be included in the price of your room

Being billed for any medications you brought with you to the hospital

Your insurance has not been applied to the bill if applicable

The next thing you need to do is to negotiate your bills with the original providers. You can do this once you have gotten any issues on the bills resolved, have seen how much will be paid by your insurance if you have any, and have a concrete idea of how much you can reasonably pay on the remaining balance.

Call each medical provider that you received a bill from and explain your situation and ask what they can do for you. Many times, they will be willing to settle for a smaller amount in order to get some money rather than none. If you are having trouble negotiating, there are professional medical bill negotiators that can help. Paying someone to help might be a hit to your finances in the short term but can ultimately save you thousands of dollars.

The statute of limitations can be restarted. A collection agency can do this by having you make a payment. Doing so will re-age the debt since the statute of limitation starts from the last payment. Then you will have to deal with the debt for another three to six years. Make sure you come to an agreement that is satisfactory to you before making payments.

Collection agencies buy debts for a fraction of what they are worth. You can use this knowledge to your advantage by offering to pay a much lower amount than you were originally billed since the collection agency will still make a profit. Ensure you are firm in the offer and obtain proof of any deal like this in writing from the agency.

Once you have settled the debt, you will receive Form 1099-C from the collection agency. This form will allow you to claim an exemption to paying the tax on the amount of the canceled debt. It is very important that you file this form with your taxes for the proper year of you can be charged taxes for money you did not have to pay.

We are not claiming that it is an ideal situation but once you have settled your debt with the collection agency, it will not affect you as much as an open, delinquent account. It will also stop debt collection calls and letters. If possible, always go for settling debts with the condition that they delete any negative account history on your credit reports.

Chapter 20: Deleting Collections and Charge-Offs

Charge Offs

Most charge offs are the result of not paying a credit card bill for several months. Typically, after 180 days of non-payments, the creditor (after hitting your credit report with several late or no payment notations) will write off the debt as a loss on their books, and cancel your account. Despite the creditor calling it a "charge-off" and taking the debt off their books, they will still want their money. Eventually, they may send it to a collection agency, or sue you if they determine that the amount is high enough.

There are several ways to fight the charge-off:

First, if you have been paying the due amount on time and the charge-off is a mistake, you have a right to demand the creditor to remove it from your credit report. See our dispute section for how to do this, but essentially you can open a dispute and it is the creditor's responsibility to prove their case against you. If they cannot prove it, then by law, they must remove it.

If the charge-off is accurate, then you still have options. To remove the charge-off, it is best to deal with it before it goes to a collection agency. In some cases, an internal department of the creditor does collections. Or the creditor may sell the owed amount to a collections company for pennies on the dollar. The collections company then hopes to collect some of the money from you and make a profit. Negotiating with a collection agency may not help since they rarely have the authority to change what has already been reported to the credit bureaus. Only the creditor can do that (the original reporter). However, even if it has already gone to a collection agency, there is a chance that you still may be able to work with the creditor.

The options are:

- You have the money and are willing to pay off the debt in full.

- You don't have the money and eventually want to pay it off or at least settle for a smaller amount.

- You don't want to pay back anything.

Late Payments

A late payment results in a delinquency mark on your credit standing. This is the most common negative item on credit reports. Items such as being 30 days late on your mortgage payment are significant, and can result in a substantial drop in your credit score. Payment history accounts for about 35% of your credit score, so late payments will have a major negative impact.

If you are currently behind on payments, ask the creditor if you can negotiate for a lower settlement amount, which includes their removing the late payments from your credit record after you have settled your debt. If they still want the full amount then you may need to catch up before you can do anything else. If you cannot pay back your late payments, ask the creditor if you can work out a new payment plan that includes removal of the late payment information after you finish making a set number of payments, such as the first twelve monthly payments for the next year.

If they still want the full amount first, then you will have to get up to date on the amount owed. Once you are up to date with your payments, you can contact the creditor and plead your case to remove the negative late payment information. If you have a long term relationship with them, let

154

them know. If you have a short term relationship with them, focus on your good record up until the current situation. Your goal is to convince them that you are a good customer and want to remain a good customer. Be polite and calm, and ask that they remove the negative information they placed on your credit record. If they agree, get the agreement in writing. Their contact information is located on your credit report under "Creditor Contacts."

Once a late payment gets on your credit report, it may remain there for up to 7 years. However, if paid in full, it may just say "paid" on your credit report.

Collections

An account is usually sent to collections six months after the first missed payment, and will remain on your credit report for up to 7 years. If you pay off the full amount owed, the account status will change on your credit report to "paid collection." If you settle for less, the account status may say "settled for less than full balance."

Unfortunately, just paying off an account that has been sent to collections will probably not help your credit score since it will still remain on your credit report.

On the positive side, the new FICO scoring system now ignores collection accounts if the original amount was under $ 100. Also, Vantage Score followed FICO's lead and now ignores all collections under $ 250. While a collection agent may still try to collect from you, these smaller amounts will no longer negatively affect your credit score. So how can you get rid of a collections account on your credit report? First: dispute it!

If the creditor or the collections agent cannot prove you owe the debt within 30 days of opening the dispute, they must remove it from your credit report. Disputing is particularly effective for collections because it is common practice for collectors to buy and sell collections accounts. If the collection agency differs from the one that is reported on your credit report, you can dispute it, and you will often win.

Second: Negotiate with the creditor and offer payment in exchange for removing the collections account from your credit report. Every creditor is different in how they respond to this. A lot depends on the creditor's employee with whom you are working. Some creditors just want their money and will cooperate with you. Most of the techniques mentioned above in "Late Payments" will also apply here as well.

Third: Ask the creditor for a "goodwill deletion" if the debt has been paid. Give them the reasons why the account went to collections. Remind them that you have been a good customer and hope that they will make a goodwill gesture and remove the collections from your credit report.

How to Deal with Harassing Collection Agencies

Generally, creditors sell debts owed to them to collection agencies when they believe it is unlikely that they themselves will be able to collect the debt. This is usually after a few months of non-payment on the delinquent account. The collections agency will buy the debt for pennies on the dollar, believing they can collect enough from you to make a profit.

In most states there is a statute of limitations for collecting debt. Usually four to five years, but you should contact your state attorney general for your specific state. If the statute of limitations has run out, the collections agency is no longer eligible to sue you. If they do anyway, it will likely be thrown out of court. If you know your debt has expired under the statute of limitations, and the collections agency contacts you, you should send them a letter explaining that you believe this is a legally uncollectable debt.

BONUS: 15 Credit Dispute Letters that Work

It is important to remember that disputing positive items on your credit report is not recommended, even if the information is wrong because it is difficult to get something placed back onto your record once it is removed. Be sure that you truly want something removed from your credit report and know what the effects of doing so will be prior to starting this process.

You will also need a hard copy of your credit report or other evidence that the error exists and copies of two forms of identification such as ID, social security card, passport, W-2 form, utility bill, or pay stub. You should mark the error on your credit report or other evidence in an obvious manner such as by circling it. Always make sure to send copies of information and keep the originals for your records.

To write a dispute letter you should:

- Use professional yet kind language that does not reflect anger or hostilities towards the credit bureaus.

- Make sure that any information you include in your letter in support of your claims cannot be used against you.

- Make your request clear and concise. Have someone you trust proofread the letter for you as well.

- Send your letter via certified mail.

- To write a dispute letter, you should not:

- Send original copies of any documents. It is crucial to have originals for your own records.

- Mention any of the laws or procedures. The credit bureaus are already aware of this information.

- State the results of court proceedings or threaten lawsuits against the credit bureaus.

Letter 1: Affidavit of unknown inquiries

EQUIFAX

P.O. box 740256

ATLANTA GA 30374

My name Is John William; my current address is 6767. W Phillips Road, San Jose, CA 78536, SSN: 454-02-9928, Phone: 415-982-3426, Birthdate: 6-5-1981

I checked my credit reports and noticed some inquiries from companies that I did not give consent to access my credit reports, I am very concerned about all activity going on with my credit reports these days. I immediately demand the removal of these inquiries to avoid any confusion as I DID NOT initiate these inquires or give any form of consent electronically, in person, or over the phone. I am fully aware that without permissible purpose no entity is allowed to pull my credit unless otherwise noted in section 604 of the FCRA.

The following companies did not have permission to request my credit report:

CUDL/FIRST CALIFORNIA ON 6-15-2017

CUDL/NASA FEDERAL CREDIT UNION ON 6-15-2017

LOANME INC 3-14-2016

CBNA on 12-22-2017

I once again demand the removal of these unauthorized inquiries immediately.

(Signature)

THANK YOU

Letter 2: Affidavit of suspicious addresses

1-30-2018

ASHLEY WHITE

2221 N ORANGE AVE APT 199

FRESNO CA 93727

PHONE: 559-312-0997

SSN: 555-59-4444

BIRTHDATE: 4-20-1979

EQUIFAX

P.O. box 740256

ATLANTA GA 30374

To whom it may concern:

I recently checked a copy of my credit report and noticed some addresses reporting that do not belong to me or have been obsolete for an extended period of time. For the safety of my information, I hereby request that the following obsolete addresses be deleted from my credit reports immediately;

4488 N white Ave apt 840 Fresno, CA 93722

4444 W Brown Ave apt 1027 Fresno CA 93722

13330 E Blue Ave Apt 189 Fresno CA 93706

I have provided my identification card and social security card to verify my identity and current address. Please notify any creditors who may be reporting any unauthorized past accounts that are in connection with these mentioned addresses as I have exhausted all of my options with the furnishers.

(Your signature)

This letter is to get a response from the courts to show the credit bureaus that you have evidence that they cannot legally validate the Bankruptcy

FIX YOUR CREDIT SCORE

Letter 3: Affidavit of James Robert

U.S BANKRUPTCY COURT

700 STEWART STREET 6301

SEATTLE, WA 98101

RE: BANKRUPTCY (164444423TWD SEATTLE, WA)

To whom it may concern:

My Name is JAMES ROBERT my mailing address is 9631 s 2099h CT Kent, WA 99999.

I recently reviewed my credit reports and came upon the above referenced public record. The credit agencies have been contacted and they report in their investigation that you furnished or reported to them that the above matter belongs to me. This act may have violated federal and Washington state privacy laws by submitting such information directly to the credit agencies, Experian, Equifax, and Transunion via mail, phone or fax.

I wish to know if your office violated Washington State and federal privacy laws by providing information on the above referenced matter via phone, fax or mail to Equifax, Experian or TransUnion.

Please respond as I have included a self-addressed envelope,

Thank You (your signature)

Letter 4: Affidavit of Erroneous entry

Dispute letter for bankruptcy to credit bureaus

1-1-18

JAMES LEE

131 S 208TH CT

KENT WA 98031

SSN: 655-88-0000

PHONE: 516-637-5659

BIRTHDATE: 10-29-1985

EXPERIAN

P. O. Box 4500

Allen, TX 75013

RE: BANKRUPTCY (132323993TWD SEATTLE, WA)

To whom it may concern:

My Name is James LEE my mailing address is 131 s 208th CT Kent, WA 98031

I recently disputed the entry of a bankruptcy that

166

shows on my credit report which concluded as a verified entry your bureau. I hereby request your methods of verification, if my request cannot be met, I demand that you delete this entry right away and submit me an updated credit report showing the changes.

Thank You (Your signature)

Letter 5: Affidavit for account validation

First letter you send to the credit bureaus for disputes

1-18-2019

TRANSUNION

P.O. BOX 2000

CHESTER PA 19016

To Whom It May Concern:

My name is John Doe, SSN:234-76-8989, my current address is 4534. N Folk street Victorville, CA 67378, Phone: 310-672-0929 and I was born on 4-22-1988.

After checking my credit report, I have found a few accounts listed above that I do not recognize. I understand that before any account or information can be furnished to the credit bureaus; all information and all accounts must be 100% accurate, verifiable and properly validated. I am not disputing the existence of this debt, but I am denying that I am the responsible debtor. I am also aware that mistakes happen, I believe these accounts can belong to someone else with a similar name or with my information used without my consent either from the furnisher itself or an individual.

I am demanding physical documents with my signature or any legally binding instruments that can prove my connection to these erroneous entries, Failure to fully verify that these accounts are accurate is a violation of the FCRA and must be removed or it will continue to damage my ability to obtain additional credit from this point forward.

I hereby demand that the accounts listed above be legally validated or be removed from my credit report immediately.

Thank You (Your signature)

Letter 6: Affidavit of request for method verification

Second letter to Credit Bureau if they verified anything

10-22-17

JOSHUA ETIIAN

2424 E Dawn Hill way

Merced, CA 93245

SSN: 555-22-3333

Phone: 415-222-9090

Birthdate: 9-29-1987

EQUIFAX

P.O. BOX 740256

ATLANTA GA 30374

To whom it may concern:

I recently submitted a request for investigation on the following accounts which were determined as verified:

Acct Numbers# (XXXXXXX COLLECTION AGENCY A)

(XXXXXXX COLLECTION AGENCY B)

I submitted enough information for you to carry out a reasonable investigation of my dispute, you did not investigate this account or account(s) thoroughly enough as you chose to verify the disputed items.

Under section 611 of the FCRA I hereby request the methods in which you verified these entries. If you cannot provide me with a reasonable reinvestigation and the methods of which you used for verification, please delete these erroneous entries from my credit report. Furthermore, I would like to be presented with all relevant documents pertaining to the disputed entries.

I look forward to resolving this manner

(Your signature)

Letter 7: Affidavit for validation

This is the first letter sent to the collection agency if the account is already on your credit reports

1-22-2017

JAMES DANIEL

13233 ROYAL LANDS

LAS VEGAS NV 89141

SSN: 600-60-0003

BIRTHDATE: 2-18-1991

PHONE: 702-331-3912

EXPERIAN

P. O. BOX 4500

ALLEN, TX 75013

To Whom It May Concern:

After reviewing my credit reports, I noticed this unknown item that you must have furnished in error, I formally deny being responsible for any parts of this debt.

Please send me any and all copies of the original

documentation that legally binds me to this account, also including the true ownership of this debt.

This account is unknown to me and I formally ask that your entity cease all reporting of this account to the credit agencies and cease all collection attempts.

ACCOUNT: UNIVERSITY OF PHOENIX (IRN 9042029892)

If you cannot present what I request, I demand you stop reporting this account to the credit bureaus to avoid FCRA and FDCPA violations and cease all contact efforts and debt collection activity.

Please respond in writing within 30 days so we can resolve this matter without any more violations.

Thank you. (Your signature)

Letter 8: Affidavit of method verification

Second letter to collection agency if they verified anything

1-30-2018

JAMES DAVID

1111 N FAIR AVE APT 101

FRESNO CA 93706

PHONE: 559-399-0999

SSN: 555-59-5599

BIRTHDATE: 9-25-1979

EXPERIAN

P. O. BOX 4500

ALLEN, TX 75013

To Whom It May Concern:

I previously disputed this account with your company and it resulted in you verifying this entry. I am once again demanding validation of this debt for the second time as I have yet to receive sufficient documentation that legally shows I am responsible for this matter.

In addition to requesting validation, I am

formally requesting your method of verification for these entries that I have previously disputed, please supply me with any documentation you may have on file to aid your stance.

If this entry cannot be validated or if the method of verification cannot be provided to me in a timely manner, I demand that you delete this entry immediately.

Thank you. (Your signature)

Letter 9: Affidavit of fraudulent information

Letter to Credit Bureau for identity theft

10-17-17

HELEN JOHNSON

2525 S CHERRY AVE APT 201

FRESNO, CA 93702

PHONE 559-299-2328

BIRTHDAY 11-30-1990

SOCIAL SECURITY NUMBER 555-89-1111

EQUIFAX CONSUMER

FRAUD DIVISION

 P.O. BOX 740256

ATLANTA GA 30374

To whom it may concern:

I am writing this letter to document all of the accounts reported by these furnishers that stem from identity theft. I have read and understand every right I have under section 605B and section 609 of the FCRA. Please block the following accounts that are crippling my consumer reports as I do not recognize, nor am I responsible for, nor have I received any money or goods from the creation of these unknown accounts.

Please refer to Police Report and ID Theft Affidavit attached.

1) CBE GROUP (12323239XXXX)

2) LOBEL FINANCIAL (431XXXX)

Please contact each credit to prevent further charges, activity, or authorizations of any sort regarding my personal information.

Thank you (Your signature)

Letter 10: Affidavit of fraudulent information

Letter to lender or collection agency when reporting fraudulent accounts

10-15-17

TARA BROWN

3421 N ROSE AVE APT 211

OAKLAND CA 93766

PHONE 559-369-9999

BIRTHDAY 9-20-1979

SOCIAL SECURITY NUMBER 584-00-0222

MONTGOMERY WARD

RE Account # 722222XXXX

TRANSUNION

P.O. BOX 2000

CHESTER PA 19016

To whom it may concern:

I have recently reviewed my credit reports and found an account listed that I do not recognize. I am informing you today that you are reporting the above-mentioned account that is a result of identity theft, and continuing to report this entry will be in violation under FACTA rules and regulations.

I have never had this account MONTGOMERY WARD 99986518XXXX, I ask that you to cease all reporting and collection activity surrounding this account which is my right under section 605B of the FCRA, please refer to police report.

I ask that this information be blocked and disregarded from your accounting. Thank you for your time and I will be eagerly waiting for your response.

Thank You (Your signature)

Letter 11: Letter to Sage Stream LLC

01-06-18

DOROTHY JAYDEN

5555 S. VALENTINE AVE. APT 307

FRESNO CA 93700

PHONE 559-333-0022

BIRTHDAY 06-20-1992

SSN: 600-00-0076

EQUIFAX

P.O. BOX 740256

ATLANTA GA 30374

I wish to freeze my credit report with your company. Please acknowledge my request with a response.

Thank You, "SIGNATURE"

Letter 12: Affidavit for validation

Validation letter to a collection agency for medical debt

2-13-2018

DONA NICOLE

1611 w Chestnut Apt 226

FRESNO CA 93788

SSN: 111-30-4555

BIRTHDATE: 9-21-1977

PHONE: 559-333-8888

EQUIFAX

P.O. BOX 740256

ATLANTA GA 30374

To whom it may concern:

After reviewing my credit reports I see this item and I formally deny any responsibility of this entry, maybe you have entered it in error as I realize you are not the original creditor or owner of the account. I hereby demand that you validate this debt and conduct a full proper investigation or delete this entry.

To be clear, I have the right to have this debt validated, as I believe you are reporting this account in error. As I see that this was a medical collection, please provide me with the date of the alleged medical service, the medical provider, and the name of the patient and any contractual obligation which binds me to this debt.

If you cannot present what I request, I demand you stop reporting this account to the credit bureaus to avoid violating section 623a (1) A: reporting information with actual knowledge of errors.

Please respond in writing within 30 days so we can resolve this matter without any more violations.

Thank you (Your signature)

Letter 13: Affidavit for validation

CHLOE MICHAEL

6350 LAUREL CANYON BLVD FL 4

NORTH HOLLYWOOD CA 91606

PHONE NUMBER: 389-324-4278

Date of Request: 06/30/2009

TRANSUNION

P.O. BOX 2000

CHESTER PA 19016

This letter was sent in response to a personal loan company that required the debtor to call in annually to renew their ACH information. But, the lender is supposed to remind the customer, in this example, they did not remind the customer and so a 30-day late payment was hit to his credit reports because the ACH did not renew. This was on an account that was over 10 years old with perfect credit history

Thank You, "SIGNATURE"

Letter 14: Complaint and Demand Letter

OLIVIA MADISON

601 N.W. Second Street

Evansville, IN 47708-1013

5-12-2018

EXPERIAN

P. O. BOX 4500

ALLEN, TX 75013

To whom it may concern:

Hello, we would like to offer One Main Financial the opportunity to correct a reckless and negligent malfeasance against customer (Since 2006) caused by One Main employees.

Recently we were notified that a negative missed payment was reported to all major credit bureaus against You, which reduced his credit score over 200 points, originating from the One Main account.

This account was set up in 2006 for the purpose of servicing a small balance to increase credit score, and has been this way up to present day.

You will see that the balance has always remained very low, with no interruptions. The account was set up on ACH several years ago.

Recently, the automatic ACH expired and no communication as received from One Main to renew the ACH. Because of the expiration of the ACH, the account went into a 30-day late period, in which finally I was notified by One Main, and he instructed One Main to immediately renew the ACH in April 2018.

The customer agent spoke with was very unhelpful regarding this situation, and stated that there was no negative credit reported since it was within 30 days. Efforts were made to explain to One Main that the ACH error is One Main's negligence, and that I never received any communication to renew or remind him of the renewal of ACH.

This same customer agent (In April) assured me that the ACH was now renewed on the same checking account. Unfortunately, this agent made a mistake and set up on an old expired account number from when the account was owned by Spring Leaf.

This technical error seems highly reckless, negligent and borderline suspicious. Thus, the ACH did not go through, unbeknownst to me and the delinquency continued into May, in which I FINALLY received another call on May 10th, in which a debt collector at One Main explained what happened, that the prior agent in April used the wrong account but there was nothing he could do about but that there is NO reason to believe that negative credit was reported.

Any person of average intelligence would see that this account had a perfect history of payment ($25 per month for many years). We believe that because the account has been transferred to so many owners (HFC, Spring Leaf and now One Main) that this has caused inaccurate data in your database and customer management systems.

This would also lead one to believe, based on these mistakes, that there may even be issues with your security of information. Cyber security vulnerabilities have also been proven to start with database and CRM weaknesses. This is clearly a broad violation of Fair Credit acts.

We strongly ask that someone at One Main investigate this case immediately, see the details for your-selves and remove the missed payment from all 3 major bureaus **immediately**. If this is not accommodated, we have no choice but to claim our rights and allegations under Federal Question.

By reporting false data to the major bureaus, I have lost my rights to a large private financial interest which requires an excellent credit standing to maintain. So the seriousness of our complaint and demand go well beyond this "courtesy" letter.

Thank you for your co-operation.

Sincerely

(Signature)

Letter 15: Pre-Litigation complaint

LIAM MASON

Address: 12395 FIRST AMERICAN WAY

POWAY CA 92064

PHONE NUMBER: 457-333-0132

Date of Request: 10/19/2018

TRANSUNION

P.O. BOX 2000

CHESTER PA 19016

(There are attachments)

To whom it may concern:

Attached is a pre-litigation complaint and demand to a collection company that [ISP] retains for unpaid debts.

Our dispute and claim is that this debt was never brought to our attention, if it is even valid, and they never made any attempt to update their billing address even though the defendant Liam had an active RESIDENTIAL account with [ISP] when these alleged claims for debts were made earlier this year at an old address. IN ADDITION, THE LAST ACCOUNT was closed and paid over the phone with a customer service representative in February of this year, so we do not even recognize or agree with the debt claim.

THIS IS in dispute and we are preparing a possible claim under Federal Question jurisdiction and the Consumer Protection Acts.

We are asking you to investigate this matter and see the error for yourself and then delete the illegal negative credit rating that [ISP] and its credit collection entity has illegally reported to you. Liam does have claims for damages he is prepared to defend and pursue if needed.

Thank you for your co-operation in this matter.

Sincerely,
(Signature)

Conclusion

In the times we live in, it is almost impossible to live without having at least one credit. The unstable rates of unemployment can affect everyone, which is why more and more Americans are confronted with the problem of bad credit. The unfortunate fact is that more and more people choose to do nothing about it and live with bad credit for a long time. What you have to understand is that bad credit gets even worse over time as its grave consequences will be felt more and more, leading to things such as the impossibility to get a new credit, refinance an old credit, rent an apartment or get a job. This is why you should take action in a time and take care of your finances, especially in the context of a shaky national and international economy.

Fixing your credit is the best solution and should become more popular in the United States, because I think it can really make a difference for a great number of people. Credit repair might seem complicated to some and it definitely takes time to finalize, but nothing great is ever accomplished without a little bit of work. Also, there is no specialist that can claim that a credit repair done in one way or another has a one hundred percent success rate. If they do, be careful with people trying to scam you for money while claiming they are repairing your bad credit.

The benefits of fixing your credit might reveal themselves over an extended period of time but by carefully doing all the steps describes in this book you will eventually clear your credit and increase your chances of you ending up with increased scores on a credit application. It will also help you with finding a job, even though your credit is not entirely repaired. When someone is evaluating your credit report and sees the written statements and all the work you have put in for the process, it shows how responsible and preoccupied you are about your finances and says a lot about who you are.

Remember to be consistent and make sure to rid yourself of all the unnecessary expenses that you have. Try to establish a new and fresh way to keep track of your payments. Do not be afraid to take action, for it is only then that you will be able to see the result. Always think positive, and don't let failure hold you back from your goal to be credit worthy once again. In the end, all the efforts are truly worth it. Not only will you have peace of mind and feel better about your life, but the more important goal is to have a trouble-free process in acquiring a new house or car because of your good and trustworthy credit. What's more, because of that good credit standing, you might even land the job or start the business that you have been dreaming of. Isn't that something to look forward to?

Many people become enthusiastic about credit repairing and when they see the effort involved and the time required on the journey to good credit, they get discouraged and give up. Others give up after the first negative response from a creditor or credit report agency and some even go through with it but stop doing things to improve their credit when they've finished the process and still haven't managed to fix all the negative items. Damage control is just as important as the process itself and, as I have said in the section of the book dedicated to this subject, it has many future benefits. The important thing about the whole process is to stay motivated and continue improving.

Make sure that you're paying attention to your credit. It's going to be extremely important throughout your life so that you can have fun and do the things you enjoy. In order to make the most of it just make sure that you're following the tips in this book and contacting a professional if you continue to have problems with your ability to stay on track and on budget.

CPSIA information can be obtained
at www.ICGtesting.com
Printed in the USA
BVHW041521171120
593515BV00012B/795